INTRODUCING THE

USA

A CULTURAL READER

MILADA BROUKAL
PETER MURPHY

Longman

Introducing the USA: A Cultural Reader

Longman, 10 Bank Street, White Plains, N.Y. 10606

Associated companies:
Longman Group Ltd., London
Longman Cheshire Pty., Melbourne
Longman Paul Pty., Auckland
Copp Clark Pitman, Toronto

Photo credits: Credits appear on page 92.

Distributed in the United Kingdom by Longman Group
Ltd., Longman House, Burnt Mill, Harlow, Essex CM20
2JE, England and by associated companies, branches,
and representatives throughout the world.

Acquisitions director: Joanne Dresner
Development editor: Kathy Sands Boehmer
Production editor: Janice L. Baillie
Text design: Pencil Point Studio
Cover design adaptation: Joseph DePinho
Cover photos: Top row, left to right: A/P Wide World Photos, Grucci, Brookhaven, NY,
    Perkins School for the Blind, Watertown, MA; center row, left to right: Washington, D.C.,
    Convention & Visitors Association, Anacostia Museum, Smithsonian Institution, Smithsonian
    Institution; bottom row, left to right: National Park Service, Courtesy of the New York
    Knicks, National Park Service
Text art: Woodshed Productions
Photo research: Polli Heyden
Production supervisor: Anne Armeny

Library of Congress Cataloging in Publication Data

Broukal, Milada.
    Introducing the USA : a cultural reader / Milada Broukal, Peter
Murphy.
       p. cm.
    ISBN 0-8013-0984-0
    1. Readers—United States. 2. United States—Civilization—
Problems, exercises, etc. 3. English language—Textbooks for
foreign speakers. I. Murphy, Peter, 1947–   II. Title.
PE1127.H5B69   1993
428.6′4—dc20   92-35468
                                                      CIP

ISBN: 0-8013-0984-0

1 2 3 4 5 6 7 8 9 10-AL-9796959493

CONTENTS

INTRODUCTION

Introducing the USA is a beginning reader for students of English as a Second Language. Twenty-eight units introduce typically American people, places, and things. A host of facts presented in the units will not only provide students with information about the USA, but will also stimulate cross-cultural exchange. The vocabulary and structures used in the text have been carefully controlled at a beginning level, while every effort has been made to keep the language natural.

Each unit contains:
- Prereading questions and introductory visuals
- A short reading passage
- Topic-related vocabulary work
- Comprehension of main ideas
- Comprehension of details
- Grammar
- Discussion questions

The prereading questions are linked to the visual on the first page of each unit. They focus the student on the topic of the unit by introducing names, encouraging speculation about content, involving the students' own experience when possible, and presenting vocabulary as the need arises.

The reading of each passage should, ideally, first be done individually by skimming for a general feel for content. The teacher may wish to deal with some of the vocabulary at this point. A second, more detailed individual reading could be done while working through the vocabulary exercise. Further reading(s) could be done aloud with the teacher or with the class.

The VOCABULARY exercise is designed to help students become more self-reliant by encouraging them to work out meaning from context. As suggested previously, this section can be done during the reading phase or afterwards or both. As in all exercise sections, a variety of exercise types is used.

There are two COMPREHENSION exercises: *Looking for Main Ideas* should be used in conjunction with the text to help students develop their reading skills, and not as a test of memory. In each case, the students are asked to confirm the basic content of the text, which they can do either individually, or in pairs, in small groups, or as a whole class. *Looking for Details* expands the students' exploration of the text, concentrating on the skimming and scanning skills necessary to derive maximum value from reading.

GRAMMAR focuses on aspects of the language suggested by the reading passage itself. The emphasis is on practice and reinforcement rather than teaching, while indirectly building on the comprehension phase.

DISCUSSION gives the students the opportunity to bring their own knowledge and imagination to the topics and related areas. They may wish to discuss all of the questions in their small groups or to select one on which to report back to the class.

THE FIFTY STATES

Unit 1

How many states can you name?
Can you find them on the map?

The fifty states of the United States, or the USA, join to make one nation. The United States did not always have fifty states. At first there were thirteen. As the United States grew, more states joined the union. The last two states to join were Alaska and Hawaii. They both joined in 1959.

The area of the United States covers every type of land. There are forests, deserts, mountains, and flat land. The area of the United States also covers every type of climate. The size of each state is different too. Alaska is the biggest state. Rhode Island is the smallest state. Alaska is 500 times bigger than Rhode Island.

About 250 million people live in the United States. The people of the United States come from all over the world. People often name cities after where they come from. For example, in the United States you find Paris, Rome, Delhi, and Frankfurt. The state with the highest population is California. The state with the lowest population is Alaska.

Each state has its own name. The name gives the state its identity and personality. More than half the states have names from American Indian origin. Each state also has a flag with colors that have a special meaning for the state. The flag is the emblem, or the symbol, of the state. There is also a state flower, tree, and bird.

VOCABULARY

Replace the underlined words in the sentences with the words below.

nation	union	origin	flat land
emblem	climate	its identity	population

1. The United States is a <u>country</u> of fifty states.

2. The United States grew, and more states joined the <u>group</u>.

3. The United States has forests, deserts, mountains, and <u>land which is level and not high</u>.

4. The United States also has every type of <u>weather</u>.

5. The state with the highest <u>number of people</u> is California.

6. More than half the states have names from American Indian <u>beginnings</u>.

7. The flag is the <u>symbol</u> of the state.

8. The name gives the state <u>a name to say what it is</u>.

COMPREHENSION

A. Looking for Main Ideas

Circle the letter of the best answer.

1. The United States _____ .
   a. was always fifty states
   b. has fifty states today
   c. is not a nation of fifty states

2. The United States has _____ .
   a. about 250 million people
   b. people from Europe and India only
   c. the highest population in the world

3. Each state has _____ .
   a. an American Indian name
   b. no personality
   c. its own name and flag

B. Looking for Details

One word in each sentence is *not* correct. Cross out the word and write the correct answer above it.

1. There is a state flag, mountain, tree, and bird.

2. Hawaii is 500 times bigger than Rhode Island.

3. More than half the states have people from American Indian origin.

4. The state with the lowest population is Hawaii.

5. Each state has a flag with colors that have a special meaning for the nation.

6. People often name states after where they come from.

GRAMMAR

Complete the sentences with the correct article. Use *the* or *a*. If no article is necessary, write **X**.

EXAMPLE: The fifty states of the United States, or ____the____ USA, make one nation.

1. _____ Alaska is the biggest state.

2. Rhode Island is _____ small state.

3. The state with the highest population is _____ California.

4. _____ people of the United States come from all over the world.

5. _____ last two states joined in 1959.

6. _____ Hawaii was a state in 1959.

DISCUSSION

Discuss the answers to these questions with your classmates.

1. Why did the states join together to form a union?
2. Find out the flag, tree, bird, and flower of the state you are in. Do you know any others?
3. Invent the fifty-first state. Why is it good for the United States if this state joins? Why is it good for this state to join the United States?

THE BUFFALO

What kind of animal is in the picture?
Where do you see buffalo?
How big do you think the buffalo is?

The buffalo is the largest North American animal. It weighs as much as 2,000 pounds. It lives with other buffalo in groups or herds. Two hundred years ago, there were 60 million buffalo. They lived all over the center of North America. There were thousands of herds. One herd was twenty miles long and twenty miles wide. The buffalo followed the grass and the Indians followed the buffalo.

The Indians used the buffalo for many things. They used it for meat. Sometimes they ate fresh meat. Sometimes they dried the meat in the sun. Then they ate it later. The Indians also used the skin, or hide, of the buffalo. From the hide they made tents, clothes, shoes, hats, and rope. They wasted nothing. But times changed.

People from other lands came to America. These immigrants crossed the country in wagon trains. They killed the buffalo for food and hides. More and more people came. And everyone wanted leather. Hunters with guns killed the buffalo only for their hides. They wasted everything else. These hunters were very good at their job. By 1900, there were fewer than thirty buffalo alive.

Today, there are about 30,000 buffalo in America. But herds are very small. You can see them in states like Wyoming. Sometimes you can buy buffalo meat at a restaurant. But you will never see a herd of buffalo as big as a city.

VOCABULARY

What is the meaning of the underlined words? Circle the letter of the correct answer.

1. The buffalo lives in herds.
   - **a.** grass
   - **b.** groups
2. The Indians used the hide of the buffalo.
   - **a.** skin
   - **b.** meat
3. Immigrants came to America.
   - **a.** People from other lands
   - **b.** People who do not like animals
4. The buffalo followed the grass.
   - **a.** saw
   - **b.** went after
5. Hunters killed the buffalo.
   - **a.** People who follow and kill animals
   - **b.** People who like restaurants
6. They wasted everything else.
   - **a.** did not like
   - **b.** did not use

COMPREHENSION

A. Looking for Main Ideas

Write the questions to these answers.

1. Where _____ ?
   The buffalo lived all over the center of North America.

2. Who _____ ?
   Hunters killed the buffalo for their hides.

3. How many _____ ?
   There are about 30,000 buffalo in America today.

B. Looking for Details

Circle T if the sentence is true. Circle F if the sentence is false.

	True	False
1. The buffalo weighs as much as 200 pounds.	T	F
2. Two hundred years ago, there were 30,000 buffalo.	T	F
3. The buffalo followed the Indians.	T	F
4. In 1900, there were fewer than thirty buffalo.	T	F
5. Hunters killed the buffalo for their hides.	T	F
6. You cannot eat buffalo meat in a restaurant today.	T	F

GRAMMAR

Complete the sentences with the prepositions below.

in	to	for	with	of

EXAMPLE: You can see buffalo _____in_____ states like Wyoming.

1. Two hundred years ago, there were many herds _____ buffalo.

2. The Indians used the buffalo _____ meat.

3. The buffalo lives _____ other buffalo.

4. The Indians used the hide _____ the buffalo.

5. The Indians dried the meat _____ the sun.

6. Immigrants came _____ America.

DISCUSSION

Discuss the answers to these questions with your classmates.

1. What other animals do people use for food and clothing?
2. How were the buffalo important to the Indians?
3. Why is the story of the buffalo important today?

TEXAS

Unit 3

What do you see in the picture?
What do you know about Texas?

A long time ago Texas was part of Mexico. The Mexican government did not want any Americans to move to Texas. But a man named Stephen Austin brought a lot of people to Texas. They built towns. The Mexican government was not happy and a war began. The Americans did not want to be part of Mexico. Many years passed. Finally, Texas was free. It became a state in 1836.

Texans are proud of their history. Many people from Mexico live in Texas today. They are an important part of the state's history. A popular kind of food in Texas is called "Tex-Mex." This means that it is a mixture of American and Mexican food.

Texas is also famous for its cowboys. These cowboys rode horses and took care of the cattle. They wore big hats and high-heeled boots. When people think of Texas, they often think of cowboys.

One way to describe Texas is "big." In fact, Texas is the second biggest state. Only Alaska is bigger. Texas has more cattle and sheep than any other state. It has the most farms or ranches in the United States. It has the biggest ranch in the country, too. Texas also produces the most fruit and vegetables. And it gives the United States one-third of American oil! That's why Texans "think big."

VOCABULARY

Complete the sentences with one of the following words.

mixture	Texan	proud	ranch
produce	describe	probably	boots

1. A person who is from Texas is a _____ .

2. A big farm with cattle on it is a _____ .

3. When you say what something is like, you _____ it.

4. When you grow something or supply something, you _____ it.

5. When you put different things together, you have a _____ .

6. When something gives you pleasure or satisfaction, you are _____ of it.

7. When there is a good chance of something, or it is likely, it will _____ happen.

8. Shoes that cover your ankles are _____ .

COMPREHENSION

A. Looking for Main Ideas

Circle the letter of the best answer.

1. Texas was _____ .
   a. a part of Mexico
   b. always part of the United States
   c. the capital of Mexico

2. Texans _____ .
   a. have no history
   b. never ride horses
   c. are proud of their history

3. To describe Texas, Texans say it is _____ .
   a. big
   b. not very big
   c. the size of a big ranch

B. Looking for Details

Circle T if the sentence is true. Circle F if the sentence is false.

	True	False
1. Texans fought against the Mexicans.	T	F
2. Texas became a state in 1836.	T	F
3. There were cowboys in Texas.	T	F
4. Americans wanted to be part of Mexico.	T	F
5. Alaska is bigger than Texas.	T	F
6. Texas gives the United States all of its oil.	T	F

GRAMMAR

Complete the sentences using the past tense form of the verbs in parentheses.

EXAMPLE: Texas _____was_____ part of Mexico.
                          (be)

1. Cowboys _____ horses on the ranches.
               (ride)

2. Stephen Austin _____ people to live in Texas.
                        (bring)

3. The cowboys _____ very big hats.
                     (wear)

4. Cowboys _____ care of the cattle.
                (take)

5. Texas _____ a state in 1836.
             (become)

6. Stephen Austin _____ towns in Texas.
                        (build)

DISCUSSION

Discuss the answers to these questions with your classmates.

1. What do you know about cowboys?
2. What special work clothes can you name?
3. An oil company found oil in your backyard. What will you do?

PEANUT BUTTER

What do you see in the picture?
Do you eat peanut butter?

Americans love to eat peanut butter. But what is peanut butter? It is a thick, creamy paste. You buy it in a jar at the grocery store. Manufacturers roast peanuts and take off the skin. Then they grind them into a thick paste—that's peanut butter!

The peanut is not really a nut, but a pea. It is a strange pea because it grows underground. But peanut plants also have green vines with yellow flowers. These vines or stems grow above the ground and are quite long. Peanuts are very healthy for you. They have more protein than a steak and they have many vitamins, too.

The peanut comes from South America, but peanut butter is a food that is truly "American." Peanut butter started in 1890 in St. Louis. A doctor made some peanut butter. He gave it to patients who could not eat regular food. Later, peanut butter was popular as a health food.

Peanut butter is very popular with children in the United States. Perhaps their favorite way to eat it is in a sandwich. Many children add jelly to their peanut butter sandwiches. This makes a favorite snack or lunchtime meal.

VOCABULARY

Complete the sentences. Circle the letter of the correct answer.

1. Peanut butter is a thick _____ .
   a. paste
   b. jelly

2. You can buy peanut butter in a _____ .
   a. skin
   b. jar

3. To make peanut butter, manufacturers _____ peanuts, and then grind them.
   a. eat
   b. roast

4. Peanut butter is healthy for you because it has _____ and vitamins.
   a. steak
   b. protein

5. Children like to eat peanut butter and _____ sandwiches.
   a. jelly
   b. butter

6. In 1890 a doctor gave peanut butter to his _____ .
   a. manufacturers
   b. patients

COMPREHENSION

A. Looking for Main Ideas

Circle the letter of the best answer.

1. Peanut butter is _____ .
   a. a thick, creamy paste
   b. jelly in a jar
   c. a sandwich

2. The peanut is a _____ .
   a. nut
   b. pea
   c. kind of steak

3. Peanut butter started _____ .
   a. in South America
   b. underground
   c. in 1890, in St. Louis

B. Looking for Details

One word in each sentence is *not* correct. Cross out the word and write the correct answer above it.

1. You buy peanut butter in a nut.

2. A favorite meal is a peanut butter and snack sandwich.

3. Peanuts are very regular for you.

4. Peanut butter started in 1980.

5. Peanut butter is a nut that is truly "American."

6. Peanut butter is very popular with patients in the United States.

7. In 1890 a manufacturer made some peanut butter and gave it to patients.

8. Manufacturers grind peanuts into a thick sandwich.

GRAMMAR

Complete the sentences with the prepositions below.

from	in	for	into

EXAMPLE: Peanut butter started _____in_____ 1890.

1. You can buy peanut butter _____ a jar.

2. Manufacturers grind peanuts _____ a paste.

3. Peanuts are healthy _____ you.

4. Peanuts come _____ South America.

5. Some Americans eat peanut butter _____ sandwiches.

6. Children like to eat peanut butter and jelly sandwiches _____ lunch.

DISCUSSION

Discuss the answers to these questions with your classmates.

1. What are the favorite children's foods in your country?
2. What other things do American children like to eat?
3. List five foods that are good for you and five foods that are bad for you.

THE PRESIDENT OF THE UNITED STATES

Unit
5

Who is the president of the United States?

Do you know the names of other U.S. presidents?

What are they famous for?

Do you want to be president of the United States of America? Maybe you can apply for the job. Answer these three questions. Are you a U.S. citizen? Are you thirty-five years old or older? Have you been a resident of the United States for fourteen years or longer? Did you say "yes" to all three questions? Then you can take the first steps to the White House.

You become president for a term. A term is four years. You can only serve two terms. This means that you can only be president twice. This became law in 1951. Before that, the law was different. In fact, Franklin D. Roosevelt became president in 1933. He was still president when he died in 1945. He was president for twelve years. No one was president longer than he was.

As president of the United States, you earn $200,000 a year. You also get an extra $50,000 for expenses, tax free. You have your own limousine, jet, and housekeepers, all free. You also live rent free, in the White House in Washington, D.C. And you are head of the richest country in the world.

Presidents of the United States are very different people. Twenty-two were lawyers, four soldiers, four farmers, four teachers, two writers, two businessmen, one engineer, one tailor, and one actor. Eight of them did not have a college education!

VOCABULARY

Replace the underlined words in the sentences with the words below.

term	resident	serve	expenses
earn	a limousine	U.S. citizen	in fact

1. To be president, you must be a <u>person who lives</u> in the United States for fourteeen years.

2. To be president, you must be a <u>person whose country is the United States.</u>

3. You become president for a <u>fixed period of time.</u>

4. A president can only <u>work for</u> two terms.

5. When you are president, you <u>make</u> $200,000 a year.

6. You also get $50,000 for <u>money to pay for other things you need.</u>

7. As president, you get free use of <u>an expensive car with a driver.</u>

8. Before 1951, you could be president for more than eight years. <u>In truth,</u> Franklin D. Roosevelt was president for twelve years.

COMPREHENSION

A. Looking for Main Ideas

Write complete answers to these questions.

1. How long can you be president for?

_____

2. How much do you earn as president of the United States?

_____

3. How many presidents were lawyers?

_____

B. Looking for Details

One word in each sentence is *not* correct. Cross out the word and write the correct answer above it.

1. To be president, you must be forty-five years old or older.

2. To be president, you must be a lawyer in the United States for fourteen years.

3. A term is eight years.

4. Franklin D. Roosevelt was president for two terms.

5. Eight presidents did not have a teacher education.

6. As president, you are the businessman of the richest country in the world.

GRAMMAR

Make these sentences plural.

EXAMPLE: One president was a lawyer.

Twenty-two _presidents were lawyers._____

1. One president was a soldier.

   Four _____

2. One president was a writer.

   Two _____

3. One president was a businessman.

   Two _____

4. One president did not have a college education.

   Eight _____

5. He was president of the United States.

   They _____

DISCUSSION

Discuss the answers to these questions with your classmates.

1. What makes a good president? Who is your favorite president? Why?
2. Can a woman be president?

MARTIN LUTHER KING, JR. Unit 6

Who is the man in the picture?
What is he famous for?

Martin Luther King, Jr., was a black clergyman from Atlanta, Georgia. When King was a child, he learned that black people and white people did not mix in public places. Black people sat in different parts of restaurants and movie theaters. Black people sat at the back of the bus. Black and white children went to different schools. This kind of separation is called *segregation*.

King loved to study. He was a good student and went to college at a young age. He was only fifteen years old. When he finished college, he began to fight segregation. He did not believe in violence. He believed in peace. He helped black people to protest in peace. They went on marches in peace.

King also wanted equality for everybody. He wanted black and white men and women to have an equal chance in the United States. This is called the *civil rights movement*. In 1963, King was the leader of the civil rights march on Washington, D.C. Thousands of people listened to his famous speech. It begins, "I have a dream."

In 1964, Martin Luther King, Jr., was the youngest person to get the Nobel Peace Prize. This award is for people who try to make peace in the world. In 1968, an assassin killed King. He was only thirty-nine years old. His birthday, January 15, is a national holiday in the United States.

VOCABULARY

Complete the sentences with one of the following words.

clergyman	violence	marches
assassin	protest	equality

1. Martin Luther King, Jr., was a Christian preacher. He was

   a _____ .

2. A person who kills a politician or leader like King

   is an _____ .

3. King told black people to complain about their situation. He told

   them to _____ .

4. He also told large numbers of black people to walk from one place
   to another to show that they were not happy. He told them to go

   on _____ .

5. King believed in peace. He did not believe

   in _____ .

6. King wanted everybody to have the same rights. He

   wanted _____ for everybody.

COMPREHENSION

A. Looking for Main Ideas

Circle the letter of the best answer.

1. In King's time, the South had _____ .
   a. segregation
   b. white buses
   c. children's restaurants

2. Civil rights is _____ .
   a. equality for everybody
   b. to be white
   c. equality for women only

3. January 15 is _____ .
   a. the day King died
   b. the day King got the Nobel Prize
   c. a national holiday

B. Looking for Details

Circle T if the sentence is true. Circle F if the sentence is false.

		True	False
1.	King did not want to stop segregation.	T	F
2.	Martin Luther King, Jr., believed in peace.	T	F
3.	In 1968, King got the Nobel Peace Prize.	T	F
4.	King died when he was thirty-nine years old.	T	F
5.	His famous speech begins, "I had a dream."	T	F
6.	In 1963, he was the leader of a civil rights march.	T	F

GRAMMAR

Complete the sentences with the prepositions below.

at	in	to	of	for

EXAMPLE: Black people sat ____in____ different parts of restaurants.

1. Black and white people did not mix _____ public places.

2. Black people sat _____ the back of the bus.

3. Martin Luther King, Jr., did not believe _____ violence.

4. Thousands of people listened _____ his famous speech.

5. King wanted equality _____ everybody.

6. He was the leader _____ the civil rights march.

DISCUSSION

Discuss the answers to these questions with your classmates.

1. What other famous people do you know who loved peace?
2. People in the United States are free. What do we mean by this?
3. Why do people follow leaders?

BASKETBALL

What are the people in the picture doing?
How do you play basketball?

James Naismith invented basketball in 1891. Naismith was a Canadian, but lived in the United States. He was a teacher at Springfield Training School in the state of Massachusetts. He taught sports and found there were no interesting games to play indoors in the winter months. So he thought of a game.

Naismith's students played the first game of basketball in the Springfield gym in 1891. There were nine men on each team. They used a soccer ball. They put peach baskets on the gym wall. The goal or purpose of the game was to throw the ball in the basket. That is why he called the game basketball. A man with a ladder went to the basket. He climbed the ladder and took the ball out of the basket. Luckily, only one man got the ball into the basket in the first game.

Basketball is a very fast game. Players must run up and down the basketball court or gym floor the whole game. At the same time they must control the ball. Today, most players are tall. Many of them are over seven feet tall and weigh more than 200 pounds. But one of basketball's great players was Barney Sedran. He played from 1912 to 1926 and is in the Basketball Hall of Fame. He was only 5 feet 4 inches tall and 118 pounds!

Today, basketball is an international sport. In America, the National Basketball Association (NBA) has some of the best players in the world. Basketball is also an Olympic sport today. In the Olympics, the best teams from many countries play to show they are the best.

VOCABULARY

Complete the definitions. Circle the letter of the correct answer.

1. A hall with ropes and bars for gymnastics and sports is a _____ .
   a. gym   **b.** school   **c.** basketball

2. A group of people who play together is a _____ .
   a. game   **b.** team   **c.** ladder

3. Another word for inside a building is _____ .
   a. winter   **b.** olympics   **c.** indoors

4. A sport that people play in every country in the world is _____ .
   a. Canadian   **b.** international   **c.** fast

5. The name of a fruit which is round and juicy is a _____ .
   a. peach   **b.** ball   **c.** basket

6. Basketball players run up and down the _____ .
   a. basket   **b.** court   **c.** ball

7. You can have a _____ of basketball, soccer, football, and tennis.
   a. pound   **b.** game   **c.** play

8. To get something high, you climb a _____ .
   a. ball   **b.** peach basket   **c.** ladder

COMPREHENSION

A. Looking for Main Ideas

Circle the letter of the best answer.

1. James Naismith _____ .
   a. invented a gym
   b. invented basketball
   c. liked peaches

2. The first game of basketball _____ .
   a. had peach baskets
   b. was like soccer
   c. was in Canada

3. Today, basketball is _____ .
   a. not an Olympic sport
   b. only played in the United States
   c. an international sport

B. Looking for Details

One word in each sentence is *not* correct. Cross out the word and write the correct answer above it.

1. There were ten men on each team.

2. They used a gym ball.

3. Naismith was American.

4. They put peach balls on the gym wall.

5. Barney Sedran was one of basketball's first players.

6. Players must climb up and down the court the whole game.

GRAMMAR

Complete the sentences with the prepositions below.

in	with	on	of	up	from

EXAMPLE: There were nine men ____*on*____ each team.

1. The first game of basketball was _____ the Springfield gym.

2. They put peach baskets _____ the wall.

3. A man _____ a ladder went to the basket.

4. The man took the ball out _____ the basket.

5. Players run _____ and down the court the whole game.

6. The best players _____ many countries play in the Olympics.

DISCUSSION

Discuss the answers to these questions with your classmates.

1. What sports can you name where you need a ball and you need to run?
2. In which sports is it an advantage to be big? In which sports is it an advantage to be small? Say why.
3. Invent a sport that you can play indoors.

ABRAHAM LINCOLN

Unit 8

Who is the man in the picture?
Why is he famous?

Abraham Lincoln was the sixteenth president of the United States. He was born in Kentucky in 1809. His family was very poor. When Lincoln was a boy, he worked on his family's farm. He did not go to school. He taught himself to read and write. Later, Lincoln studied law and became a lawyer. After that, he became a politician.

Everybody liked Abraham Lincoln because he was intelligent and hard-working. Lincoln was very ambitious. He wanted to be good at everything he did. He said that he wanted to win the "race of life." He was also kind and honest. People called him "Honest Abe."

Lincoln became president in 1860. In 1861, there was a war between the North and the South of the United States. The people in the South wanted a separate government from the United States. The North wanted the United States to stay together as one country. Lincoln was the leader of the North. In the war, brother killed brother. The Civil War was four years long.

The North won the Civil War. The war ended on April 9, 1865. Six days later, President Lincoln and his wife went to the theater. Inside the theater, a man went behind the president and shot him in the head. The man's name was John Wilkes Booth. He was a supporter of the South. Lincoln died the next morning.

VOCABULARY

Complete the definitions. Circle the letter of the correct answer.

1. When you always tell the truth, you are _____ .
   a. intelligent   **b.** honest   **c.** hard-working
2. When other people follow you, you are their _____ .
   a. brother   **b.** family   **c.** leader
3. When you want to be the best at everything, you are _____ .
   a. honest   **b.** ambitious   **c.** kind
4. When you believe in an idea or an action, you are its _____ .
   a. president   **b.** supporter   **c.** wife
5. When your job is to give advice to people about the law, you are a _____ .
   a. lawyer   **b.** politician   **c.** president
6. When you kill with a gun, you _____ .
   a. shoot   **b.** win   **c.** end

COMPREHENSION

A. Looking for Main Ideas

Write complete answers to these questions.

1. Why did everybody like Abraham Lincoln?

_____

2. When did Lincoln become president?

_____

3. Who won the Civil War?

_____

B. Looking for Details

Circle T if the sentence is true. Circle F if the sentence is false.

	True	False
1. Lincoln was born in 1860.	T	F
2. People called Lincoln "Honest Abe."	T	F
3. The war started in 1860.	T	F
4. Lincoln was the leader of the North.	T	F

	True	False
5. The war ended in 1865.	T	F
6. The Civil War was six years long.	T	F
7. Abraham Lincoln died in the war.	T	F
8. John Wilkes Booth killed Lincoln.	T	F

GRAMMAR

Complete the sentences with the prepositions below.

of	between	behind	in	on

EXAMPLE: Lincoln was president _____in_____ 1860.

1. When Lincoln was a boy, he worked _____ his family's farm.

2. There was a war _____ the North and the South.

3. The war ended _____ April 9, 1865.

4. A man went _____ the president.

5. The man shot the president _____ the head.

6. Booth was a supporter _____ the South.

DISCUSSION

Discuss the answers to these questions with your classmates.

1. Abraham Lincoln's parents were poor. Do children of poor parents make better leaders?
2. Some people look like the job they do. Pretend you do not know Abraham Lincoln. Look at his picture and guess what job he does.
3. Abraham Lincoln was honest. List the qualities that make a good president.

WASHINGTON, D.C.

What do you see in the picture?

Where are these buildings?

Can you name any other famous buildings in this city?

Washington, D.C. is the capital of the United States. It is an unusual city. It is a city that has no state. It is a district—the District of Columbia or D.C. That is why we say Washington, D.C.

George Washington became the first president of the United States in 1790. At that time the new United States had no capital city. It was necessary to have a capital city that was not a part of a state. Washington picked a place for the capital near his home, Mount Vernon. The state of Maryland gave some land and Virginia gave some land. This made the District of Columbia. The name of the capital is after George Washington.

The city of Washington, D.C. has wide streets, parks, and beautiful buildings. These buildings tell the history of the United States. The most famous building is the White House. This is the home of the president. Another important building is the Capitol. This is where Congress meets to make the laws of the country.

Washington, D.C. is very special in the spring. It is cherry blossom time. Japan sent more than 3,000 cherry trees to the United States in 1912. The trees have beautiful flowers in March or April. It is a very pretty time to see Washington, D.C.

Millions of people visit Washington, D.C. Tourism is an important business. The other business is government. Every year the president sees the leaders of many countries in Washington, D.C.

VOCABULARY

What is the meaning of the underlined words? Circle the letter of the correct answer.

1. Washington, D.C. is the capital of the United States.
   a. the city where the center of government is
   b. the biggest city

2. Washington, D.C. is an unusual city.
   a. different from other cities
   (b). not an interesting city

3. George Washington picked a place for the capital.
   (a.) thought about
   b. chose

4. The city of Washington, D.C. has wide streets.
   a. long
   (b.) large

5. It is cherry blossom time in the spring.
   (a.) the time when cherry trees have flowers
   b. the time when the cherry trees have fruit

6. Tourism is an important business in Washington, D.C.
   (a.) job
   b. pastime

COMPREHENSION

A. Looking for Main Ideas

Circle the letter of the best answer.

1. Washington, D.C. has no _____ .
   a. city
   (b.) state
   c. district

2. George Washington _____ .
   a. picked the place for the capital
   (b.) gave some land to Virginia
   c. did not want a capital city

3. The city of Washington, D.C. has _____ .
   a. the homes of all the presidents
   b. no parks
   (c.) the home of the president

B. Looking for Details

Circle T if the sentence is true. Circle F if the sentence is false.

	True	False
1. Mount Vernon was George Washington's home.	**T**	**F**
2. Virginia was not a state.	**T**	**F**
3. The Capitol is another name for the White House.	**T**	**F**
4. Congress meets in the White House.	**T**	**F**
5. Japan sent cherry trees to the United States.	**T**	**F**
6. The trees are beautiful but have no flowers.	**T**	**F**

GRAMMAR

Complete the sentences with the correct article. Use *a* or *the*. If no article is necessary, write X.

EXAMPLE: ___X___ Washington, D.C. is very special in the spring.

1. Washington, D.C. is _the_ capital of the United States.

2. Washington, D.C. is _a_ district—the District of Columbia.

3. _the_ Japan sent cherry trees to the United States.

4. The most famous building is _the_ White House.

5. It is the home of _the_ president.

6. _the_ Capitol is another important building in Washington, D.C.

DISCUSSION

Discuss the answers to these questions with your classmates.

1. Name and describe the capital city of your country.
2. What important buildings do you find in a capital city?
3. Why do people choose one city to be the capital? Is it the biggest, the richest, or is it one in the middle of the country? Can you think of other reasons?

HALLOWEEN

Describe the things you see in the picture.
What do you know about Halloween?

On October 31, Americans celebrate Halloween. Halloween means "holy" (*hallow*) "evening" (*een*). This is the evening before the Christian holy day of All Saints Day. On All Saints Day, Christians remember the saints. But Halloween is even older than Christianity.

Before Christianity, people in Europe believed that on October 31 ghosts of dead people came back. To scare the ghosts, people dressed like devils and were very noisy. They also made big fires to keep the ghosts away. Later, people did not believe in ghosts, but they kept the day of Halloween for fun.

Immigrants came from Europe to America and brought with them the custom of Halloween. Halloween has some strange symbols. One symbol is the jack-o'-lantern in the window. The jack-o'-lantern is to scare the ghosts. People cut the pumpkin, throw away all of the inside, and cut a face in it. Then they put a candle inside of it. Jack-o'-lanterns usually look scary, too!

Today, in the United States, Halloween is very popular with children. They wear masks and special costumes. They want to look like skeletons and ghosts. Then they go from house to house and say, "Trick or treat!" People give them candies, cookies, or fruit. When people give nothing, the children sometimes play tricks on them.

VOCABULARY

Replace the underlined words in the sentences with the words below.

saints	ghosts	masks
scare	play tricks	skeletons

1. On All Saints Day, Christians remember the <u>holy people</u>.

2. To <u>frighten</u> the ghosts, people dressed like devils.

3. Children wear <u>something to cover their faces</u>.

4. Children want to look like <u>all the bones that make the body</u>.

5. The jack-o'-lantern is to scare <u>the people with no bodies that come back after they die</u>.

6. When people give nothing, the children <u>do something to make them look stupid</u>.

COMPREHENSION

A. Looking for Main Ideas

Circle the letter of the best answer.

1. On October 31, Americans celebrate _____ .
   a. All Saints Day
   (b.) Halloween
   c. Christianity

2. _____ from Europe brought Halloween to America.
   a. Saints
   (b.) Immigrants
   c. Children

3. Today, Halloween is _____ .
   (a.) popular with children
   b. for people who give nothing
   c. for special people

B. Looking for Details

Circle T if the sentence is true. Circle F if the sentence is false.

	True	False

1. All Saints Day is the day before Halloween.   T   F
2. Halloween is older than Christianity.   T   F
3. Halloween came from Europe.   T   F
4. A jack-o'-lantern is a pumpkin.   T   F
5. On Halloween, children say "Trick"!   T   F
6. On Halloween, people give jack-o'-lanterns.   T   F

GRAMMAR

Complete the sentences with the prepositions below.

in	on	into	for	with	from

EXAMPLE: Immigrants came ___from___ Europe.

1. Americans celebrate Halloween ___on___ October 31st.
2. You put a jack-o'-lantern ___into___ the window.
3. A jack-o'-lantern is a pumpkin with a face cut ___with___ it.
4. Halloween is very popular ___for___ children.
5. Children go ___in___ house to house.
6. People kept the day of Halloween ___for___ fun.

DISCUSSION

Discuss the answers to these questions with your classmates.

1. Do you have a special day like Halloween in your country? How is it the same? How is it different?
2. List any U.S. holidays or special days you know. Compare your list with a friend's.
3. Do you believe in ghosts? Say why or why not.

AMERICAN INDIANS

Unit 11

Who is the man in the picture?
What do you know about American Indians?

There were about one million people in North America when Columbus arrived in 1492. Columbus thought he was in India. He called the people with dark skin *Indians*. This was a mistake, but the name *Indian* stuck.

There were more than 2,000 tribes at the time of Columbus. Each tribe had a different name. Each tribe also had a different language and customs. But all these people could speak with each other in one language—sign language. All these people also thought in the same way. They believed that the land and waters belonged to everybody.

The people who came after Columbus from Europe did not understand the first or "native" Americans. Many of them thought the Indians were savages. They were afraid of them. For the next 400 years they fought with each other. They fought about who owned the land and how to use it.

The tribes lost their land, and the U.S. government made them live on reservations. Reservations were tax free land "reserved for" the Indians. The government gave them food because they could not hunt and find food for themselves. There was no work for them. In 1924 a law made "native" Americans citizens of the United States. Today some Indian tribes choose to live by their old customs, and some do not.

VOCABULARY

Complete the sentences. Circle the letter of the correct answer.

1. Columbus called the people with _____ skin *Indians*.
   a. free
   b. dark

2. Each _____ had a different language and custom.
   a. tribe
   b. name

3. Tribes could speak with each other in _____ .
   a. water language
   b. sign language

4. People from Europe thought the first Americans were _____ .
   a. savages
   b. citizens

5. The U.S. government made the "native" Americans live on _____ .
   a. water
   b. reservations

6. Some Indian tribes choose to live by their old _____ .
   a. years
   b. customs

COMPREHENSION

A. Looking for Main Ideas

Circle the letter of the best answer.

1. Columbus thought he was in _____ .
   a. North America
   b. the United States
   c. India

2. All American Indians _____ .
   a. thought in the same way
   b. had the same customs for all tribes
   c. were one tribe

3. Many "native" Americans _____ .
   a. are not U.S. citizens
   b. live on reservations
   c. give food to the government

B. Looking for Details

Circle T if the sentence is true. Circle F if the sentence is false.

		True	False
1.	Columbus went to India.	T	F
2.	There were more than one million tribes at the time of Columbus.	T	F
3.	Each tribe had a different language.	T	F
4.	The tribes used sign language to speak with each other.	T	F
5.	Americans and Indians fought for 400 years.	T	F
6.	The "native" Americans became U.S. citizens in 1924.	T	F

GRAMMAR

Complete the sentences using the past tense form of the verbs in parentheses.

EXAMPLE: Columbus ___arrived___ in 1492.
(arrive)

1. Columbus _____ he was in India.
(think)

2. The American Indians _____ the land belonged to everybody.
(believe)

3. For 400 years they _____ with each other.
(fight)

4. The tribes _____ their land.
(lose)

5. The U.S. government _____ them food.
(give)

6. In 1924 a law _____ the Indians U.S. citizens.
(make)

DISCUSSION

Discuss the answers to these questions with your classmates.

1. What do you know about American Indians?
2. In what other countries are there tribes of people?
3. Tell your classmates about the most interesting tribe you know.

SHIRLEY TEMPLE

Who is the little girl in the picture?
Why is she famous?

Shirley Temple was born in 1928 in California. She was a very cute little girl. She had blond curly hair and dimples in her cheeks. But she was also a good actress, singer, and dancer.

By age three, Shirley was making movies and soon became a famous movie star. When she was six, she made some big movies. By the time she was eight, she was making $500,000 a year. The people who made the movies called her "Little Miss Miracle."

In the 1930s, life was difficult in the United States. Many people did not have jobs. But thousands of poor people paid money to go to the movies to watch Shirley Temple. People felt happy when she sang and danced. Mothers wanted their daughters to have curly hair like Shirley Temple. Little girls played with Shirley Temple dolls.

Everybody loved little Shirley. People sent her gifts. On her eighth birthday she got 1,000 cakes. Her fans sent her 5,000 letters a week. But her mother did not spoil her. Little Shirley only got $4.25 a week and had to eat her spinach.

When Shirley Temple grew up, she did not make any more movies. She got married to Charles Black and had two children. In the 1960s, Shirley Temple Black went into politics. In 1974, she was U.S. ambassador to Ghana, a country in Africa. Then in 1989 she was U.S. ambassador to Czechoslovakia.

VOCABULARY

Complete the sentences. Circle the letter of the correct answer.

1. Shirley Temple was a _____ little girl.
   a. cute   **b.** difficult

2. She had _____ in her cheeks.
   a. spinach   **b.** dimples

3. She had _____ blond hair.
   a. curly   **b.** happy

4. The people who made movies called her "Little Miss _____ ."
   a. Movie   **b.** Miracle

5. Her _____ sent her 5,000 letters a week.
   a. daughters   **b.** fans

6. Her mother did not _____ her.
   a. send   **b.** spoil

7. Little girls played with Shirley Temple _____ .
   a. dolls   **b.** hair

8. In the 1960s, Shirley Temple Black went into _____ .
   a. politics   **b.** dolls

COMPREHENSION

A. Looking for Main Ideas

Circle the letter of the best answer.

1. When Shirley was three _____ .
   a. she became a singer
   b. she made movies
   c. her mother was ambassador

2. In the 1930s, thousands of people _____ .
   a. sang and danced
   b. went to the movies to watch Shirley Temple
   c. had curly hair

3. When Shirley grew up, she _____ .
   a. did not get married
   b. did not make any more movies
   c. lived in Africa for the rest of her life

B. Looking for Details

Number the sentences 1 through 8 to show correct order.

_____ When she was eight, she made $500,000 a year.

_____ After that, she was U.S. ambassador to Czechoslovakia.

_____ Shirley Temple started to make movies at age three.

_____ In the 1960s, she went into politics.

_____ In 1974, she was U.S. ambassador to Ghana.

_____ At age six, she made some big movies.

_____ She got married to Charles Black and had two children.

_____ When she grew up, she did not make any more movies.

GRAMMAR

Complete the sentences using the past tense form of the verbs in parentheses.

EXAMPLE: Shirley Temple _____*had*_____ blond curly hair.
(have)

1. Shirley Temple _____ a good actress.
(be)

2. At age six, she _____ some big movies.
(make)

3. Little girls _____ with Shirley Temple dolls.
(play)

4. Everybody _____ Shirley Temple.
(love)

5. People _____ Shirley gifts.
(send)

6. Mothers _____ their daughters to have hair like Shirley.
(want)

DISCUSSION

Discuss the answers to these questions with your classmates.

1. What other famous children do you know?
2. Do you think it is good or bad to be famous when you are young?
3. Do some parents push their children to do too much?

POPCORN

What do you see in the picture?
Do you like popcorn?
What other kinds of corn do you know?

All corn does not pop. A seed or kernel of corn must have 14 percent water in it to pop. Other kinds of corn have less water and do not pop. When you put a kernel of corn on a fire, the water inside makes the corn explode. This makes a "pop" noise. That is why we call it *popcorn*.

The American Indians popped corn a long time ago. The Indians knew there were three kinds of corn. There was sweet corn for eating, corn for animals, and corn for popping. The Indians introduced corn to the first settlers, or Pilgrims, when they came to America in 1620. One year after they came, the Pilgrims had a Thanksgiving dinner. They invited the Indians. The Indians brought food with them. One Indian brought popcorn!

Since that time Americans continued to pop corn at home. But in 1945 there was a new machine that changed the history of popcorn. This electric machine popped corn outside the home. Soon movie theaters started to sell popcorn to make more money. Popcorn at the movies became more and more popular. Today, Americans still continue the custom of eating popcorn at the movies.

Americans use 500,000 pounds of popcorn every year. Many people like to put salt and melted butter on their popcorn. Some people eat it without salt or butter. Either way—Americans love their popcorn!

VOCABULARY

Complete the definitions. Circle the letter of the correct answer.

1. A thing that people in a country always do is a _____ .
   a. pop
   b. custom

2. A few is the same as _____ .
   a. several
   b. many

3. When you tell people about something for the first time,
   you _____ them to it.
   a. make
   b. introduce

4. When you ask some people if they want to do something,
   you _____ them.
   a. invite
   b. change

5. The small part of a plant that grows into a new plant is a _____ .
   a. corn
   b. seed

6. When something bursts, or pops, it _____ .
   a. explodes
   b. continues

COMPREHENSION

A. Looking for Main Ideas

Circle the letter of the correct answer.

1. For corn to pop, it must have _____ .
   a. less than 12 percent water
   b. 14 percent water
   c. no water

2. The Indians _____ .
   a. sold popcorn to the Pilgrims
   b. brought popcorn to Thanksgiving dinner
   c. did not know about popcorn

3. Today, popcorn is _____ .
   a. only popular at home
   b. popular at the movies
   c. not popular

B. Looking for Details

Circle T if the sentence is true. Circle F if the sentence is false.

		True	False
1.	The American Indians knew about three kinds of corn.	T	F
2.	Americans use 500,000 pounds of popcorn a year.	T	F
3.	The Pilgrims had a Thanksgiving dinner.	T	F
4.	The Indians invited the Pilgrims.	T	F
5.	In 1925, an electric machine popped corn.	T	F
6.	An Indian brought popcorn to the Thanksgiving dinner.	T	F

GRAMMAR

Make these sentences negative.

EXAMPLE: All corn pops.
  All corn does not pop.

1. Other kinds of corn have 14 percent water.

2. Other kinds of corn pop.

3. Popcorn pops in water.

4. Today, people eat popcorn for Thanksgiving.

5. Popcorn at the movies is popular in every country.

6. Movie theaters in the United States sell sweet corn.

DISCUSSION

Discuss the answers to these questions with your classmates.

1. What do you eat when you go to the movies in your country?
2. How do you eat corn in your country?
3. What cereal is special to your country and how do you eat it?

BEVERLY HILLS

Unit 14

What do you see in the picture?
Why is Beverly Hills famous?

Most visitors to Los Angeles, California, want to go and see Beverly Hills. This is where you find the homes of the movie stars. But Beverly Hills is not Los Angeles. It is a small city next to Los Angeles.

All kinds of celebrities live in Beverly Hills. These celebrities may be movie stars, television stars, sports stars, or other people in the news. Tourists can buy special maps for the homes of the stars. These homes are very beautiful. They usually have swimming pools and tennis courts. But sometimes you cannot see very much. The homes have high walls or trees around them.

Beverly Hills is also famous for Rodeo Drive. This is one of the most expensive shopping streets in the United States. Rodeo Drive started to be an elegant street in the 1960s. Many famous stores opened on the street. People liked all the new styles and fashions they could buy. Today, you can find the most expensive and unusual clothing, jewelry, and furniture in the world on Rodeo Drive. Rodeo Drive is a very special street. When you want to park your car in public parking, an attendant will come and park your car for you.

Beverly Hills is really a small city. Only about 35,000 people live there. But during the day more than 200,000 people come to Beverly Hills to work or to shop!

VOCABULARY

Replace the underlined words in the sentences with the words below.

celebrities	an elegant	An attendant
unusual	public parking	jewelry

1. Many <u>famous people</u> have homes in Beverly Hills.

2. On Rodeo Drive, you can buy some very <u>strange</u> and expensive things.

3. On Rodeo Drive, even <u>the place where people can park their cars for free</u> is special.

4. <u>A person who works in a parking lot</u> parks your car for you.

5. You can find expensive <u>decorations made of gold or diamonds that you wear on your clothes or body</u> on Rodeo Drive.

6. Rodeo Drive became <u>a beautiful and expensive</u> street in the 1960s.

COMPREHENSION

A. Looking for Main Ideas

Circle the letter of the best answer.

1. In Beverly Hills you find _____ .
   a. Los Angeles
   b. the homes of the movie stars
   c. the homes of tourists

2. The homes of celebrities have _____ .
   a. no trees and tennis courts
   b. maps on them
   c. swimming pools and tennis courts

3. Rodeo Drive _____ .
   a. is an expensive shopping street
   b. has no parking
   c. has only clothing stores

B. Looking for Details

One word in each sentence is *not* correct. Cross out the word and write the correct answer above it.

1. The houses have tennis stores.

2. Beverly Hills is a sports city.

3. The homes of the stars have small walls.

4. On Rodeo Drive, a celebrity will come and park your car for you.

5. About 200,000 people live in Beverly Hills.

6. Tourists can buy special jewelry for the homes of the stars.

GRAMMAR

Complete the sentences with the prepositions below.

of	in	for	around	on

EXAMPLE: Celebrities live _____ in _____ Beverly Hills.

1. Beverly Hills is where you find the homes _____ the stars.

2. Beverly Hills is famous _____ Rodeo Drive.

3. The homes have high walls _____ them.

4. Rodeo Drive is one of the most expensive streets _____ the world.

5. You can find the most expensive jewelry _____ Rodeo Drive.

6. On Rodeo Drive, a parking attendant will park your

   car _____ you.

DISCUSSION

Discuss the answers to these questions with your classmates.

1. Imagine you are a famous person and describe your home.
2. Why do so many rich people want to live in the same town?
3. You have won one million dollars. You have one hour to spend it on Rodeo Drive. What will you buy?

THEODORE ROOSEVELT

Who is the man in the picture?
Why is he famous?

Theodore Roosevelt was the twenty-sixth president of the United States. He was president from 1901 to 1909. He was a very intelligent man. He was also very energetic. He was a boxer, a soldier, a rancher, and an explorer.

This energetic man was not strong when he was a boy. He had problem with his breathing. He had asthma. His father wanted him to be strong. Roosevelt learned to box and did many other sports. Soon Roosevelt became strong and energetic.

After he became president, Roosevelt kept his body strong. He even boxed in the White House. One day, another boxer hit him in the eye. After that accident, Roosevelt became blind in one eye.

Theodore Roosevelt's nickname was "Teddy." Everybody called him Teddy. When he was president, he often went hunting. One day he went hunting with some friends and saw a small bear. He did not shoot the bear. He said the bear was too small and must go free. The next day the story of the little bear was in the newspapers. The newspapers named the little bear "Teddy" after the president. Soon people called toy bears for children "teddy bears."

When he left the White House, Teddy Roosevelt went to hunt in Africa. He then went to South America to explore places that nobody knew about. Everybody loved his energy.

VOCABULARY

Complete the sentences with one of the following words.

energetic	rancher	an explorer
asthma	nickname	to hunt

1. Theodore Roosevelt was a man who owned and worked on a very large farm. He was a _____ .

2. Roosevelt's friends did not call him Theodore. They called him "Teddy." That was his _____ .

3. A disease which makes breathing difficult at times is called _____ .

4. A person who is full of life and is very active is _____ .

5. Theodore Roosevelt liked to travel to places to discover something. He was _____ .

6. Roosevelt liked to chase and catch or kill animals for sport. He liked _____ .

COMPREHENSION

A. Looking for Main Ideas

Circle the letter of the best answer.

1. Theodore Roosevelt was _____ .
   a. not intelligent
   b. very energetic
   c. president for twenty-six years

2. Theodore Roosevelt's nickname was _____ .
   a. Teddy
   b. Teddy Bear
   c. Little Bear

3. When he was a boy, Roosevelt _____ .
   a. wanted to be president
   b. was not strong
   c. had a problem with his father

B. Looking for Details

Circle T if the sentence is true. Circle F if the sentence is false.

		True	False
1.	Theodore Roosevelt was also a rancher.	T	F
2.	When he was a boy, Theodore had asthma.	T	F
3.	Roosevelt hit a president in the eye.	T	F
4.	Roosevelt had bears in the White House.	T	F
5.	People called toy bears "teddy bears."	T	F
6.	Teddy Roosevelt went to hunt in South America.	T	F

GRAMMAR

Complete the sentences with the prepositions below.

after	in	from	to	with	for

EXAMPLE: Roosevelt boxed _____in_____ the White House.

1. Theodore Roosevelt was president _____ 1901 to 1909.

2. Roosevelt became blind _____ one eye.

3. One day he went hunting _____ some friends.

4. The newspapers named the little bear "Teddy" _____ the president.

5. People called toy bears _____ children "teddy bears."

6. Roosevelt went _____ South America.

DISCUSSION

Discuss the answers to these questions with your classmates.

1. Why do sick people often do great things?
2. What is good and what is bad about hunting?
3. Find nicknames for everyone in your group or class.

ROADRUNNERS, RATTLESNAKES AND OPOSSUMS

Describe the animals in the picture.
Can you say one special thing about each one?

THE ROADRUNNER

This strange bird gets its name because it runs along roads. It runs very fast—up to twenty miles an hour on its long legs—but it can fly too. The roadrunner is usually brown and white and has several feathers on top of its head. It is about two feet long with its long tail. Roadrunners live in the desert parts of the United States. They eat insects, and they also kill and eat snakes like the rattlesnake.

THE RATTLESNAKE

The rattlesnake is famous for the sound it makes—a rattle. When you surprise the snake, it shakes the end of its tail. This makes a sound like a rattle—a lot of quick little noises. The rattlesnake usually lives in dry parts of the United States. It can be about eight feet long, and is dangerous. It goes out at night to kill small animals. The rattlesnake has bad eyes, but it can feel the heat of an another animal from a long way.

THE OPOSSUM

The opossum is the only animal in North America that keeps its babies in a pouch, or bag, on its stomach. The opossum looks like a very big, fat mouse, except it is as big as a cat. When another animal wants to kill it, the opossum lies down, closes its eyes, hangs out its tongue, and does not move. The other animal thinks the opossum is dead and goes away.

VOCABULARY

What is the meaning of the underlined words? Circle the letter of the correct answer.

1. The roadrunner gets its name because it runs <u>along</u> roads.
   a. in the direction of
   b. across
2. The rattlesnake <u>shakes</u> its tail.
   a. feels
   b. moves
3. The rattlesnake's tail makes a sound like <u>a rattle</u>.
   a. quick little noises
   b. very big feet
4. The rattlesnake can feel the <u>heat</u> of an animal.
   a. temperature
   b. noise
5. The roadrunner is a <u>strange</u> bird.
   a. bad
   b. unusual
6. The opossum <u>keeps</u> its babies in a pouch.
   a. holds
   b. makes

COMPREHENSION

A. Looking for Main Ideas

Circle the letter of the best answer.

1. The roadrunner gets its name because it _____ .
   a. has long legs
   b. runs along roads
   c. kills snakes
2. The rattlesnake is famous for _____ .
   a. its heat
   b. its bad eyes
   c. the sound it makes
3. The opossum is the only animal in North America that _____ .
   a. keeps its babies in a pouch
   b. keeps a bag
   c. has a stomach

B. Looking for Details

Circle T if the sentence is true. Circle F if the sentence is false.

		True	False
1.	The roadrunner eats rattlesnakes.	T	F
2.	The roadrunner cannot fly.	T	F
3.	The rattlesnake is not dangerous.	T	F
4.	The rattlesnake kills at night.	T	F
5.	The opossum looks like a large mouse.	T	F
6.	The opossum keeps its tongue in a pouch.	T	F

GRAMMAR

Complete the sentences with the prepositions below.

for	on	in	out	down	away

EXAMPLE: The rattlesnake usually lives _____in_____ dry parts of the United States.

1. The opossum keeps its babies in a pouch _____ its stomach.

2. Roadrunners live _____ the desert parts of the United States.

3. The rattlesnake goes _____ at night.

4. The opossum lies _____ , and does not move.

5. The rattlesnake is famous _____ the sound it makes.

6. The other animal thinks the opossum is dead and

   goes _____ .

DISCUSSION

Discuss the answers to these questions with your classmates.

1. Can you name other birds that live mostly on the ground?
2. What kind of snakes do you know? How do they kill their food?
3. What other animals do you know that keep their babies in pouches?

HARRIET TUBMAN

Why do we say African-American?
What is a slave?

Harriet Tubman was born around 1820 in the South of the United States. She was an African-American and a slave. In those days in the South, African-Americans were slaves. People bought slaves to work in their houses, farms, and fields. Their masters bought and sold them like property. When Harriet became a young woman, she wanted to be free. She wanted to escape to the North of the United States. Everyone in the North was free.

Finally, Harriet Tubman escaped from the South to the North on the Underground Railroad. The Underground Railroad was not a real railroad. It was a secret organization of people. These people helped slaves to escape. At night, they took the slaves to a safe house. The slaves hid there. The next night, they took the slaves to the next house or "station" on the railroad. The word *underground* can mean secret. This is why people called the organization the Underground Railroad.

When Harriet Tubman was free, she decided to help slaves. So she joined the Underground Railroad. Soon she became its leader. It was a very dangerous job. She went back to the South time after time. She brought back slaves to freedom in the North. Before Harriet Tubman died in 1913, she helped 300 slaves to escape. She helped these people begin new lives as free men and women. Today, we honor the name of this brave woman.

VOCABULARY

Complete the definitions. Circle the letter of the correct answer.

1. People who were not free and were bought and sold were _____ .
   a. fields   b. slaves   c. station

2. When you pay for something and it is yours, it is your _____ .
   a. house   b. property   c. farm

3. When you run away from a place, you _____ .
   a. join   b. escape   c. call

4. The people who bought and sold slaves were called _____ .
   a. masters   b. organization   c. property

5. When you do not do something openly, it is _____ .
   a. free   b. real   c. secret

6. The slaves did not want people to see them, so they _____ .
   a. went back   b. hid   c. called

7. When you are not afraid to do something, you are _____ .
   a. dangerous   b. brave   c. safe

8. When you show respect, you _____ someone.
   a. honor   b. become   c. decide

COMPREHENSION

A. Looking for Main Ideas

Circle the letter of the best answer.

1. Harriet Tubman wanted to be _____ .
   a. a slave
   b. free
   c. an African-American

2. The Underground Railroad was _____ .
   a. a secret organization
   b. a real railroad
   c. a house in the North

3. Harriet Tubman _____ .
   a. was dangerous
   b. had slaves
   c. helped slaves

B. Looking for Details

Circle T if the sentence is true. Circle F if the sentence is false.

		True	False
1.	Harriet was born in the North of the United States.	T	F
2.	African-Americans in the South were slaves.	T	F
3.	Harriet wanted to escape to the South.	T	F
4.	*Underground* also means secret.	T	F
5.	Harriet became the leader of the Underground Railroad.	T	F
6.	Harriet helped 130 slaves to escape.	T	F

GRAMMAR

Complete the sentences using the past tense form of the verbs in parentheses.

EXAMPLE: Harriet Tubman ____was____ an African-American.
(be)

1. Around 1820 African-Americans in the South _____ slaves.
(be)

2. Masters _____ their slaves.
(sell)

3. Harriet _____ from the South.
(escape)

4. The people in the Underground Railroad _____ the slaves
to safe houses. (take)

5. The slaves _____ in the houses.
(hide)

6. Harriet _____ to help slaves.
(decide)

7. Harriet _____ the leader of the Underground Railroad.
(become)

8. Harriet _____ back to the South to help slaves.
(go)

DISCUSSION

Discuss the answers to these questions with your classmates.

1. Why is it good to be free?
2. What kind of work did slaves do?
3. What brave people can you name? What did they do?

JULY FOURTH

What do you see in the picture?
What U.S. holidays do you know?

July Fourth is the birthday of the United States. It is a national holiday. Another name for July Fourth is Independence Day. We celebrate July Fourth as Independence Day because on July 4, 1776, the original thirteen colonies declared their independence from England.

Before 1776, the King of England ruled the thirteen colonies in America. The colonists were angry with the King because of taxes. They wanted their independence from England. A war started in 1775 between the colonists and soldiers from England. The colonists won the war. They wanted to say why they wanted their independence or freedom from England. So they chose Thomas Jefferson to write the Declaration of Independence.

On July 4, 1776, the leaders of the colonies signed the Declaration of Independence in Philadelphia, Pennsylvania. It said that all people were equal and had the right to live in freedom. A new nation was born. People rang bells and fired guns for the birth of the United States of America.

Today, we celebrate July Fourth in many different ways. During the day, many people get together with friends and family members for picnics. Many cities have parades with bands in the streets. At night there are noisy fireworks. These beautiful fireworks of different colors light up the sky all across the country.

VOCABULARY

Complete the sentences. Circle the letter of the correct answer.

1. We _____ July Fourth as Independence Day.
   a. write   **b.** celebrate   **c.** get together

2. The King of England _____ the thirteen colonies.
   a. rang   **b.** chose   **c.** ruled

3. The _____ were angry with the King of England.
   a. colonists   **b.** colors   **c.** bells

4. The colonists _____ the war.
   a. signed   **b.** rang   **c.** won

5. The _____ of the colonies signed the Declaration of Independence.
   a. kings   **b.** leaders   **c.** soldiers

6. People _____ guns on July Fourth, 1776.
   a. started   **b.** wanted   **c.** fired

7. Today, on July Fourth beautiful _____ light up the sky.
   a. fireworks   **b.** guns   **c.** names

8. Many cities have _____ in the streets.
   a. colors   **b.** parades   **c.** picnics

COMPREHENSION

A. Looking for Main Ideas

Circle the letter of the best answer.

1. July Fourth is _____ .
   a. the King of England's birthday
   b. Independence Day
   c. a national holiday in every country

2. On July 4, 1776, _____ .
   a. the leaders of the thirteen colonies signed the Declaration of Independence
   b. the English won the war
   c. Thomas Jefferson was born

3. Today, on July Fourth there are _____ .
   a. fireworks at night
   b. wars in many cities
   c. colonists in the streets

B. Looking for Details

One word in each sentence is *not* correct. Cross out the word and write the correct answer above it.

1. The Queen of England ruled the thirteen colonies in America.

2. A war started between the colonists and leaders from England.

3. Thomas King wrote the Declaration of Independence.

4. People fired bells for the birth of the United States.

5. Today, on July Fourth, friends and family get together for kings.

6. At night, fireworks light up the sky all across the state.

GRAMMAR

Complete the sentences using the past tense form of the verbs in parentheses.

EXAMPLE: The King of England ___ruled___ the colonies.
(rule)

1. The colonists _____ angry with the King.
(be)

2. The colonists _____ their independence.
(want)

3. In 1775 a war _____ .
(start)

4. The American colonists _____ the war.
(win)

5. They _____ Thomas Jefferson.
(choose)

6. The leaders _____ the Declaration of Independence.
(sign)

DISCUSSION

Discuss the answers to these questions with your classmates.

1. What is your favorite national holiday? How do people celebrate your favorite national holiday?
2. For what reasons do countries have national holidays?
3. Invent a national holiday and tell what it is for and how to celebrate it.

THE SEQUOIAS

How tall do you think the tree in the picture is?
How old do you think it is?

The sequoia trees are the oldest living things in the world. You can find them only in the north of California. They are huge. Some are over 250 feet high. Many sequoias are over 3,000 years old. They are living giants.

The name *sequoia* comes from Sequoyah, an American Indian. Sequoyah developed an alphabet for his people, so they could read and write.

The bark, or outside part of the sequoia, has a special tannin or juice. This protects the tree from fire and insects. So sequoias never die from fire or disease.

The biggest sequoia is the General Sherman tree. This tree is 100 feet around its base, or bottom. It is 267 feet tall. This means it is about the same size as a building with twenty-six floors. It is also the oldest tree in the world. The General Sherman tree is 4,000 years old!

When people needed wood, they began to cut down the sequoias. John Muir was a famous naturalist. He studied plants and animals. Muir wanted to save the sequoias. He asked President Theodore Roosevelt to come and see the sequoias in California. The president came, and in 1903 he made the land where they grew into a national park—Sequoia National Park.

VOCABULARY

Complete the definitions. Circle the letter of the correct answer.

1. Something that is very, very big is _____ .
   a. huge   **b.** high   **c.** tall

2. The bottom of a tree is its _____ .
   a. bark   **b.** base   **c.** juice

3. A person who studies plants and animals is a _____ .
   a. sequoia   **b.** nationalist   **c.** naturalist

4. The thick outside part of a tree is the _____ .
   a. tannin   **b.** bark   **c.** juice

5. Something that is much bigger than normal is a _____ .
   a. giant   **b.** building   **c.** world

6. When something saves you from bad things, it _____ you.
   a. protects   **b.** finds   **c.** studies

7. When something is sick, it may have a _____ .
   a. fire   **b.** bark   **c.** disease

8. Sequoyah made an alphabet for his people. He _____ it especially for them.
   a. saved   **b.** grew   **c.** developed

COMPREHENSION

A. Looking for Main Ideas

Circle the letter of the best answer.

1. The sequoia trees are _____ .
   a. the oldest living things in the world
   b. died 3,000 years ago
   c. the oldest things in the world

2. The General Sherman tree is _____ .
   a. not the oldest sequoia
   b. the biggest and oldest sequoia
   c. the tallest sequoia

3. President Roosevelt _____ .
   a. cut down sequoias
   b. saved John Muir
   c. made Sequoia National Park

B. Looking for Details

One **word in each sentence is** *not* **correct. Cross out the word and write the correct answer above it.**

1. Sequoia trees are the oldest living things in California.

2. Some Sequoias are 250 feet old.

3. The General Sherman tree is 100 feet around its tannin.

4. Sequoyah developed an American for his people.

5. The bark of the sequoia has a special fire.

6. John Muir was a famous president.

7. Muir wanted to save the people.

8. President Roosevelt made the land where the sequoias grew into a presidential park.

GRAMMAR

The words in the sentences are not in the correct order. Rewrite the sentence with the words in the correct order.

EXAMPLE: the / General Sherman / old / is / tree / 4,000 years

The General Sherman tree is 4,000 years old.

1. naturalist / was / a / John Muir / famous

_____

2. General Sherman / around / the / is / 100 feet / its / tree / base

_____

3. has / bark / a / the / juice / special

_____

4. to / sequoias / Muir / wanted / save / the

_____

5. disease / sequoias / from / fire / never / die / or

_____

6. plants / John Muir / studied / and / animals

_____

DISCUSSION

Discuss the answers to these questions with your classmates.

1. What other names of trees do you know?
2. What do people use wood for?
3. Why are scientists worried about people cutting down forests?

HELEN KELLER

Who is the person in the picture?
What is she famous for?
Do you know any deaf or blind people?

Helen Keller was born in Alabama in 1880. When she was twenty months old, she got an illness. After her illness Helen could not hear or see. She was deaf and blind. Helen was a difficult child. Her parents did not know what to do.

Finally, when Helen was seven years old, her parents got her a special teacher. Her name was Miss Anne Sullivan. Miss Sullivan worked with Helen all day. She took Helen's hand and spelled a word in her hand. Helen soon learned to say what she wanted in this way.

In 1900 Helen entered Radcliffe College. Miss Sullivan sat next to Helen in class. She spelled all the words into Helen's hand. Miss Sullivan also read to Helen all the time. At that time there were only a few books for the blind. These were Braille books. They had a special alphabet made with dots that blind people could read with their fingers. Helen graduated from Radcliffe with honors, or very high grades.

Helen wrote books like *The Story of My Life* and *Midstream—My Later Life*. She also wrote magazine articles and spoke all over the country. She learned to speak. It was not easy to understand her. Miss Sullivan repeated what Helen said. Helen spoke about the deaf and blind. People everywhere became interested. There was new hope for the deaf and blind.

VOCABULARY

Complete the sentences with one of the following words.

deaf	blind	Braille	graduate
honors	an article	repeat	an illness

1. When a person cannot see, he or she is _____ .

2. When a person cannot hear, he or she is _____ .

3. The special alphabet made with dots for people who cannot see is called _____ .

4. A piece of writing in a newspaper or magazine is _____ .

5. When you complete your degree in a college or university, you _____ .

6. When you say something again for the second time, you _____ it.

7. A sickness or a disease is _____ .

8. When a student is excellent in her studies, he or she graduates with _____ .

COMPREHENSION

A. Looking for Main Ideas

Circle the letter of the best answer.

1. When Helen was a baby, she _____ .
   a. became blind
   b. became deaf and blind
   c. could not hear

2. Helen had _____ .
   a. a special teacher
   b. old parents
   c. one hand

4

3. Helen Keller _____ .
   a. read only two books
   b. did not finish college
   c. graduated from college

5.

3. Helen's teacher was Miss Sullivan.

B. Looking for Details

Number the sentences 1 through 8 to show the correct order.

_____ She got a special teacher when she was seven.

_____ In 1900 she entered Radcliffe College.

_____ When she was twenty months old she became deaf and blind.

_____ Helen Keller was born in 1880.

_____ Helen graduated from college with honors.

_____ Helen spoke about the deaf and blind everywhere.

_____ Her teacher's name was Anne Sullivan.

_____ Miss Sullivan sat next to Helen in class and spelled the words in her hand.

GRAMMAR

Complete the sentences using the past tense form of the verbs in parentheses.

EXAMPLE: In 1900 Helen ___*entered*___ Radcliffe College.
(enter)

1. Miss Sullivan _____ with Helen all day.
(work)

2. Miss Sullivan _____ Helen's hand.
(take)

3. Helen _____ to speak.
(learn)

4. Miss Sullivan _____ what Helen said.
(repeat)

5. Miss Sullivan also _____ to Helen all the time.
(read)

6. Helen _____ magazine articles and books.
(write)

DISCUSSION

Discuss the answers to these questions with your classmates.

1. What famous deaf or blind people do you know?
2. What are the problems when you are deaf and blind?
3. What do we do today to help handicapped people?

NEW YORK CITY

What do you see in the picture?
What do you know about New York?

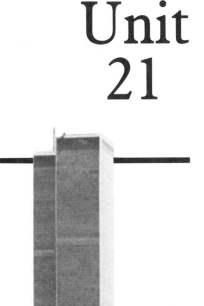

New York is the largest city in the United States. More than seven million people live there. New York has very tall buildings like the World Trade Center and the Empire State Building. It is the biggest port in the world. Thousands of ships come to the port of New York each year. It has Macy's, one of the biggest stores in the world. New York also has the largest lady in the world—the Statue of Liberty.

New York is a very cosmopolitan city. People from many countries came to live in New York. Three-quarters, or 75 percent, of the people in New York City come from five groups. The groups are: blacks, Jews, Italians, Puerto Ricans, and Irish. The other quarter, or 25 percent, comes from all over the world.

New York City is the center for culture in the United States. It has the finest museums and best art galleries in the country. If you want to see a play, there are many theaters you can go to on Broadway. The street called Broadway is the center for theater in the United States.

People call New York City the "Big Apple." Jazz musicians in the 1920s gave New York this name. When a musician says he is going to the Big Apple, it means he is the best. Today, New York is still the U.S. center for art and business.

VOCABULARY

Complete the definitions. Circle the letter of the correct answer.

1. A town with a harbor where ships can stop is a _____ .
   a. center   **b.** port   **c.** store

2. A city where there are people from different parts of the world is _____ .
   a. cosmopolitan   **b.** Irish   **c.** tall

3. With its many art galleries, museums, and theaters you can see that New York is the center for _____ in the United States.
   a. business   **b.** ships   **c.** culture

4. You go to the theater to see _____ .
   a. a gallery   **b.** jazz   **c.** a play

5. When you cut something into four parts, each part is a _____ .
   a. quarter   **b.** center   **c.** three quarters

6. When something is of the best quality, it is the _____ .
   a. largest   **b.** finest   **c.** biggest

COMPREHENSION

A. Looking for Main Ideas

Circle the letter of the best answer.

1. New York _____ .
   a. has the largest ladies in the United States
   b. is the largest city in the United States
   c. is a tall city

2. New York is _____ .
   a. a black and Irish city
   b. a cosmopolitan city
   c. three-quarters Puerto Rican

3. New York _____ .
   a. has galleries on Broadway
   b. has only museums
   c. is the center for culture in the United States

B. Looking for Details

One word in each sentence is *not* correct. Cross out the word and write the correct answer above it.

1. More than eleven million people live in New York City.

2. Three-quarters of the people in New York come from four groups.

3. The street called Liberty is the center for theater.

4. Jazz musicians in the 1960s called New York the "Big Apple."

5. Macy's is one of the biggest ships in New York.

6. Thousands of plays come to the port of New York each year.

GRAMMAR

Complete the sentences with the correct article. Use *a* or *the*. If no article is necessary, write *X*.

EXAMPLE: New York is __*a*__ cosmopolitan city.

1. New York is _____ biggest port in the world.

2. _____ Statue of Liberty is in New York.

3. People call _____ New York City the "Big Apple"

4. New York is _____ a large city.

5. New York has tall buildings like _____ World Trade Center.

6. You can see _____ play on Broadway.

DISCUSSION

Discuss the answers to these questions with your classmates.

1. Which is your favorite big city? Describe it.
2. Do you like to live in a big city? Say why.
3. Describe the big city of your dreams.

ICE-CREAM SUNDAE

What do you see in the picture?
What kind of ice cream do you like?
Do you like ice-cream sundaes?

The ice-cream sundae is an original American dish. Ice cream is not an original American food and chocolate syrup is not an original American food. But an American put the two together and started the ice-cream sundae.

An ice-cream sundae is ice cream with chocolate or other syrup over it. There are many kinds of toppings today. You put the toppings on top of the syrup. These can be nuts, fruit, and whipped cream.

Ice-cream sundaes started in the 1890s. At that time people went to ice-cream parlors to eat ice cream. One day in Wisconsin a customer went to an ice-cream parlor. He wanted chocolate syrup on his vanilla ice cream. The owner of the parlor said this was a bad idea. But the customer insisted and finally got what he wanted. Soon many customers wanted syrup on their ice cream. Other ice-cream parlors started to have this new ice-cream dish.

The sundae got its name from an ice-cream parlor in another town in Wisconsin. Here the owner of an ice-cream parlor only served the unusual ice-cream dish on Sundays. The ice-cream with the syrup was a special order and it was more expensive. It was a Sunday special. That is how it got the name sundae. Nobody knows why the spelling changed from Sunday to sundae.

VOCABULARY

Complete the definitions. Circle the letter of the correct answer.

1. A special store where you go to just eat ice cream is an
   ice-cream _____.
   a. parlor   **b.** Sunday   **c.** ice

2. _____ is a thick, sweet liquid.
   a. nuts   **b.** Syrup   **c.** vanilla

3. Cream that is light and airy is _____ .
   a. whipped   **b.** chocolate   **c.** original

4. Something you put on top of food is _____ .
   a. a cream   **b.** fruit   **c.** a topping

5. When you offer food, you _____ it.
   a. know   **b.** start   **c.** serve

6. A special kind of food that you prepare is a _____ .
   a. name   **b.** sundae   **c.** dish

7. When something is yours, you are the _____ .
   a. idea   **b.** owner   **c.** special

8. The person who goes to a store to buy something is the _____ .
   a. owner   **b.** customer   **c.** people

COMPREHENSION

A. Looking for Main Ideas

Circle the letter of the best answer.

1. An ice-cream sundae is ice cream with _____ .
   a. vanilla
   b. chocolate or other syrup
   c. food

2. The ice-cream sundae started _____ .
   a. with fruit
   b. in the 1890s
   c. with no ice cream

3. The name sundae came from _____ .
   a. Sunday
   b. the name of the customer
   c. the name of the owner

B. Looking for Details

Circle T if the sentence is true. Circle F if the sentence is false.

		True	False
1.	The man who started the ice-cream sundae was an American.	T	F
2.	You can have many kinds of toppings.	T	F
3.	In the 1790s people went to ice-cream parlors.	T	F
4.	The ice-cream sundae started in Wisconsin.	T	F
5.	The customer wanted chocolate syrup over his chocolate ice cream.	T	F
6.	Soon customers wanted fruit on their ice cream.	T	F

GRAMMAR

Complete the sentences with the prepositions below.

in	from	with	on	to

EXAMPLE: You put the toppings ____*on*____ top of the syrup.

1. An ice-cream sundae is ice cream _____ chocolate syrup.

2. People went _____ ice-cream parlors to eat ice cream.

3. Soon many customers wanted syrup _____ their ice cream.

4. The owner only served the unusual ice cream _____ Sundays.

5. The ice-cream sundae started _____ Wisconsin.

6. The spelling changed _____ Sunday to sundae.

DISCUSSION

Discuss the answers to these questions with your classmates.

1. What ice-cream dishes do you like?
2. What flavors of ice cream can you name?
3. Invent a new ice-cream dish.

THOMAS ALVA EDISON

Who is the man in the picture?
Where do you think he is?
What is he famous for?

Thomas Alva Edison was born in 1847. He was sick a lot when he was young. Edison's mother taught him lessons at home and he only studied the things he wanted to know. At age ten, he read his first science book. After he read the book, he built a laboratory in his house. Soon, Edison started to invent things. He was interested in the telegraph and electricity. At age twenty-three, he made a special telegraphic machine and sold it for a lot of money. With this money, he was now free to invent all the time.

Edison started his own laboratory at Menlo Park, New Jersey. He hired mechanics and chemists to help him. He worked day and night. Once, he worked on forty-five inventions at the same time. Edison did not sleep very much, but he took naps. He often fell asleep with his clothes on. One day, he even fell asleep in a closet!

Did you know Edison invented wax paper, fire alarms, the battery, and motion pictures? But his favorite invention was the phonograph, or record player. He invented the phonograph in 1876. His other famous invention was the light bulb. Edison died in 1931, at the age of eighty-four. He had over 1,300 inventions to his name! Many people say that Edison was a genius—one of the smartest people in the world!

VOCABULARY

Complete the sentences with one of the following words.

invent	closet	laboratory
hired	nap	light bulb

1. Edison liked to _____ things.

2. Edison worked in his _____ day and night.

3. When you take a short sleep, it is a _____ .

4. A place where you hang your clothes is a _____ .

5. Edison paid chemists and mechanics to work for him.

   He _____ them.

6. When the lamp in your house does not work, you may need to

   change the _____ .

COMPREHENSION

A. Looking for Main Ideas

Circle the letter of the best answer.

1. When Edison was a boy, he _____ .
   a. made a lot of money
   b. built a laboratory in his house
   c. invented motion pictures

2. In his laboratory at Menlo Park, Edison _____ .
   a. worked day and night
   b. slept most of the time
   c. did not work

3. Edison invented _____ .
   a. only a record player
   b. his name
   c. more than 1,300 things

B. Looking for Details

Number the sentences 1 through 7 to show the correct order.

_____ He died in 1931, at the age of eighty-four.

_____ With this money he started to invent.

_____ Edison was ten when he read his first science book.

_____ In 1876, he invented the phonograph.

_____ After that, he built a laboratory in his house.

_____ When he was twenty-three, he made a lot of money.

_____ He started his own laboratory at Menlo Park.

GRAMMAR

Complete the sentences with the past tense forms of the verbs in parentheses.

EXAMPLE: Edison ___*started*___ his own laboratory in Menlo Park.
(start)

1. Edison _____ the light bulb.
(invent)

2. When he was twenty-three, he _____ a special machine.
(make)

3. He _____ this invention for a lot of money.
(sell)

4. Edison _____ chemists to help him.
(hire)

5. Edison _____ day and night.
(work)

6. He often _____ naps.
(take)

DISCUSSION

Discuss the answers to these questions with your classmates.

1. What other famous inventors or scientists do you know?
2. What invention(s) do you want to see in the future?
3. Do you know other people who do not sleep very much at night, but take naps in the day?

THE PENTAGON

Unit 24

How many sides does the building in the picture have?

Who do you think works in the building?

The Pentagon is a building in Arlington, Virginia, near Washington, D.C. It has the offices of the U.S. Department of Defense. The Department of Defense includes the Army, Navy, Air Force, Marines, and Coast Guard.

The word *pentagon* comes from the Greek *penta*, which means "five." A pentagon is a figure with five sides. Look at the picture. The Pentagon has five rings. The rings are inside each other. Each ring has five sides. How tall do you think the Pentagon is? The answer is easy. Each ring is five stories tall.

The Pentagon is the largest office building in the world. It has seventeen miles of halls. People can get lost in the Pentagon. So the walls on each floor are a different color (brown, green, red, gray, and blue). This helps people to know where they are. There are also many maps in the halls!

The Pentagon is so big that it is like a city. Almost 30,000 people work there. The Pentagon has its own doctors, dentists, and nurses. It has its own banks and stores. It has a post office, a fire department, and a police department. It also has an important center for communications. This center guards the country. It is hundreds of feet under the ground. The Pentagon even has its own radio and TV stations.

VOCABULARY

Replace the underlined words in the sentences with the words below.

figure	rings	stories	includes
maps	Navy	get lost	halls

1. A pentagon is a <u>shape</u> with five sides.

2. The building has seventeen miles of <u>long corridors or passageways</u>.

3. The Pentagon is five <u>floors</u> high.

4. Sometimes people <u>cannot find their way</u> in the Pentagon.

5. In the Department of Defense, there is the Army, <u>the country's war ships and people who work on them</u>, Air Force, Marines, and Coast Guard.

6. The Pentagon has five <u>circles</u> which are inside each other.

7. To help you know where you are, you look at <u>plans</u> of the building.

8. The Department of Defense <u>contains</u> the Army, Navy, Air Force, Marines, and Coast Guard.

COMPREHENSION

A. Looking for Main Ideas

Circle the letter of the best answer.

1. The Pentagon has the offices of _____ .
   a. the U.S. Department of Defense
   b. the Army
   c. the Navy and the Air Force

2. The Pentagon has five _____ .
   a. halls
   b. sides
   c. offices

3. The Pentagon _____ .
   a. has the longest halls in the world
   b. has walls of different colors on the same floor
   c. is the largest office building in the world

B. Looking for Details

Circle T if the sentence is true. Circle F if the sentence is false.

		True	False
1. The Pentagon is in Washington, D.C.		T	F
2. The Department of Defense includes the Army, Navy, Air Force, Marines, and Coast Guard.		T	F
3. The greek word *penta* means "five."		T	F
4. The Pentagon has seventy miles of halls.		T	F
5. The colors of the floors are red, blue, green, white, and gray.		T	F
6. The Pentagon has its own police department.		T	F

GRAMMAR

Complete the sentences with the prepositions below.

of	on	in	with	near

EXAMPLE: You can get lost __in__ the Pentagon.

1. The Pentagon is _____ Washington, D.C.

2. The Pentagon has the offices _____ the U.S. Department of Defense.

3. The walls _____ each floor are a different color.

4. A pentagon is a figure _____ five sides.

5. There are maps _____ the halls.

6. The Pentagon is the largest building _____ the world.

DISCUSSION

Discuss the answers to these questions with your classmates.

1. What are the good and bad points of working in such a big place?
2. What other government building can you name in the United States?
3. Draw a picture of the soldier of the future. Then describe his or her uniform and equipment.

JAIME ESCALANTE

Describe the man in the picture.
Why do you think he is famous?
Who is your favorite teacher?

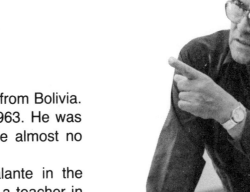

Jaime Escalante was a teacher from Bolivia. He arrived in Los Angeles in 1963. He was thirty-three years old and spoke almost no English.

Life was difficult for Escalante in the United States. He could not be a teacher in California. He had to go to college again. It took him many years, but he did it. He worked at a restaurant to support his family at the same time.

Finally, when he was forty-three he started to work at Garfield High School in Los Angeles. This school had a bad name. There were many gangs and the students were not doing well. Soon Escalante changed things.

Escalante worked with his students. He taught them math. He used his own methods, or ways, and they worked. The students learned and enjoyed their math. In 1982, fourteen of his students passed an advanced math examination. Nobody believed this. People said the students were cheating. The students wanted to show they were not cheating. They took the exam again. And they passed again. This was a miracle in a place like Garfield! This was the work of Jaime Escalante.

Every year Escalante produced top class students. People know him as one of the best teachers in America. There is even a movie and a book about him.

VOCABULARY

Complete the sentences. Circle the letter of the correct answer.

1. Jaime Escalante worked in a restaurant to _____ his family.
   a. enjoy
   b. support

2. There were many _____ at Garfield High School.
   a. gangs
   b. families

3. Nobody believed the students passed the exam. This was a _____ at Garfield!
   a. work
   b. miracle

4. Nobody believed the students passed the exam. People said the students were _____ .
   a. cheating
   b. arriving

5. Escalante used his own _____ .
   a. movies
   b. methods

6. Every year Escalante _____ top students.
   a. learned
   b. produced

COMPREHENSION

A. Looking for Main Ideas

Circle the letter of the best answer.

1. Jaime Escalante _____ .
   a. came to the United States in 1963
   b. spoke good English when he arrived in the United States
   c. was thirty-three when he arrived in Bolivia

2. When he was forty-three, Escalante started to _____ .
   a. change his name
   b. work at Garfield High School
   c. do bad things

3. People think Escalante is one of the _____ .
   a. top students in his class
   b. best students in a movie
   c. best teachers in America

B. Looking for Details

Circle T if the sentence is true. Circle F if the sentence is false.

		True	False
1.	At thirty-three Escalante started to teach at Garfield High School.	T	F
2.	Escalante taught math.	T	F
3.	Garfield High School was in Los Angeles.	T	F
4.	In 1982, fourteen students at Garfield High School did not pass the math exam.	T	F
5.	There were no gangs at Garfield High School.	T	F
6.	There is a movie about Jaime Escalante.	T	F

GRAMMAR

Complete the sentences using the past tense form of the verbs in parentheses.

EXAMPLE: Escalante ___*arrived*___ in Los Angeles in 1963.
(arrive)

1. Escalante _____ almost no English.
(speak)

2. At forty-three, Escalante _____ to work at Garfield High School.
(start)

3. His students _____ their math.
(enjoy)

4. Fourteen of his students _____ the math exam in 1982.
(pass)

5. Nobody _____ the students passed the exam.
(believe)

6. People _____ the students were cheating.
(say)

DISCUSSION

Discuss the answers to these questions with your classmates.

1. How do you think Escalante changed his students?
2. Which are your favorite school classes? Which are you best at? Why?
3. Discuss what makes a good teacher and what makes a good student.

CHEERLEADERS

Unit 26

Who do you see in the picture?
What are they doing?

When you go to a college or high school sports event, you see cheerleaders. Cheerleaders are male and female. They dress in the colors of their team. They jump and dance in front of the crowd and shout the name of their team. Their job is to excite the crowd. Everybody makes a lot of noise. They want their team to win the game.

The first cheerleader was a man. In 1898, Johnny Campbell jumped in front of the crowd at the University of Minnesota and shouted for his team. He shouted, "Hoo-rah Minn-e-so-tah!" This was the first organized shout, or "yell." For the next thirty-two years cheerleaders were men only. Women were not cheerleaders until 1930.

Today cheerleaders work in teams. They practice special shouts, dances, and athletic shows. Often the women work separately from the men. But cheerleaders are most exciting when men and women work together. The men throw the women high in the air and catch them. The team members climb on each other's shoulders to make a human pyramid. They yell and dance too. It is like human fireworks.

Cheerleaders now have their own contests. Every year there are local, state, and national contests for cheerleaders. The best teams make new, faster, and more exciting shows to be the best. And the crowd shouts. They want their cheerleaders to win.

VOCABULARY

What is the meaning of the underlined words? Circle the letter of the correct answer.

1. At a college or high school sports <u>event</u>, you see cheerleaders.
   a. race or competition
   b. dance

2. Cheerleaders dress in the colors of <u>their team</u>.
   a. the group of teachers they support
   b. the group of sports people they support

3. The job of cheerleaders is to <u>excite the crowd</u>.
   a. make the crowd have strong feelings
   b. make the crowd calm

4. Cheerleaders <u>yell</u> and dance.
   a. sing
   b. shout

5. Often the women work <u>separately</u> from the men.
   a. apart
   b. with

6. Cheerleaders climb on each other's shoulders and make a human <u>pyramid</u>.
   a. shape which is square at the bottom and meets at a point at the top
   b. shape which is round

7. Cheerleaders have their own <u>contests</u>.
   a. costumes
   b. competitions

8. Every year there are contests which are <u>local</u>.
   a. in the area where they live
   b. very important

COMPREHENSION

A. Looking for Main Ideas

Write complete answers to these questions.

1. Where do you see cheerleaders?

   _____

2. Who was the first cheerleader?

   _____

3. How do cheerleaders work today?

   _____

B. Looking for Details

One word in each sentence is *not* correct. Cross out the word and write the correct answer above it.

1. Cheerleaders dress in the color of their pyramid.

2. Cheerleaders jump and dress in front of the crowd.

3. Cheerleaders want their team to win the dance.

4. Cheerleaders are girls and women.

5. Men were not cheerleaders until 1930.

6. In 1898, Johnny Campell jumped in front of the pyramid.

GRAMMAR

Complete the sentences with the prepositions below.

in	from	on	of	for	until

EXAMPLE: They dress _____ in _____ the color of their team.

1. Cheerleaders work _____ teams.

2. They jump and dance in front _____ the crowd.

3. Women were not cheerleaders _____ 1930.

4. The women work separately _____ the men.

5. They climb _____ each other's shoulders.

6. There are local and national contests _____ cheerleaders.

DISCUSSION

Discuss the answers to these questions with your classmates.

1. Do you think that cheerleaders are a good idea?
2. What do people wear and carry to show support for their team?
3. What noises do people make to show support for their team?

YELLOWSTONE NATIONAL PARK

Unit 27

What do you see in the picture?
Do you know a place like this?

A national park is a large piece of land. In the park animals are free to come and go. Trees and plants grow everywhere. People go to a national park to enjoy nature. Many people stay in campgrounds in national parks. They sleep in tents and cook their food over campfires. They also walk on trails or paths in the parks. On a gate at the entrance of Yellowstone, a sign says, "For the Benefit and Enjoyment of the People."

Yellowstone is the world's oldest national park. It became a national park in 1872. It is also the world's largest park. It covers parts of the states of Wyoming, Montana, and Idaho. Yellowstone is two-and-a-half times the size of the smallest state, Rhode Island.

Yellowstone is famous for its geysers. These holes in the ground shoot hot water into the air. There are about seventy geysers in the park. The most famous is Old Faithful. About every hour Old Faithful shoots hot water hundreds of feet into the air.

Two-and-a-half million people visit this beautiful park each year. Park rangers give information to visitors. They also take care of the park. They tell visitors not to pick the flowers. They also tell them not to feed or hunt the animals.

VOCABULARY

Complete the sentences. Circle the letter of the correct answer.

1. People go to a national park to enjoy _____ .
   a. people   **b.** nature

2. There is a sign on a _____ .
   a. visitor   **b.** gate

3. The sign says, "For the _____ and Enjoyment of the People."
   a. Benefit   **b.** Information

4. Yellowstone is famous for its _____ .
   a. visitors   **b.** geysers

5. Park rangers _____ of the park.
   a. feed   **b.** take care

6. Visitors cannot _____ the animals.
   a. hunt   **b.** pick

COMPREHENSION

A. Looking for Main Ideas

Write complete answers to these questions.

1. Why do people go to a national park?

   _____

2. When did Yellowstone become a national park?

   _____

3. How many people visit Yellowstone each year?

   _____

B. Looking for Details

Circle the letter of the best answer.

1. Yellowstone covers parts of _____ .
   a. Wyoming and Montana   **b.** Wyoming, Montana, and Idaho

2. Yellowstone is two-and-a-half times the size of _____ .
   a. Montana   **b.** Rhode Island

3. Yellowstone has about _____ .
   a. twenty geysers   **b.** seventy geysers

4. Geysers shoot hot water into the _____ .
    a. ground   **b.** air

5. The most famous geyser is _____ .
    a. Old Faithful   **b.** Old Hundred

6. Park rangers give _____ to visitors.
    a. flowers   **b.** information

GRAMMAR

Make these sentences plural.

EXAMPLE: This hole in the ground shoots hot water into the air.
> *These holes in the ground shoot hot water into the air.*

1. There is a geyser.

_____

2. There is a national park.

_____

3. A park ranger gives information to a visitor.

_____

4. A park ranger takes care of the park.

_____

5. A national park is a large piece of land.

_____

6. A ranger tells a visitor not to pick the flower.

_____

DISCUSSION

Discuss the answers to these questions with your classmates.

1. Where do you prefer to go in your free time—to the mall, the mountains, or the beach? Say why.
2. What kinds of parks do you know?
3. Do you think national parks are a good idea?

THE STARS AND STRIPES Unit 28

How many stripes are there on the flag?
What do you think the stars stand for?

The "Stars and Stripes" is a popular name for the red, white, and blue flag of the United States. Another popular name is the "Star Spangled Banner." This is also the name of the national anthem of the United States.

Every country has its own flag. In 1776, the thirteen colonies declared their independence from Great Britain. The United States was born. George Washington was the general of the American Army. He decided that the United States needed a flag, too.

There is a story that General George Washington asked Betsy Ross to make the flag. She used three colors: red, white, and blue. The color red was for courage, white was for liberty, and blue was for justice. She sewed thirteen red and white stripes and thirteen white stars in a circle on a blue square. The thirteen stars and stripes stood for the number of states at the beginning of the United States. On June 14, 1777, Congress voted this flag to be be the national flag.

Later, new states joined the United States. This was a problem for the flag. In 1818, Congress made another law about the flag. The thirteen stripes stayed the same, but for each new state there was a new star. Today, there are fifty stars on the flag. Hawaii was the last star in 1959.

VOCABULARY

Complete the definitions. Circle the letter of the correct answer.

1. A national song of a country is called the national _____ .
   a. flag   **b.** star   **c.** anthem

2. Another word for freedom is _____ .
   a. white   **b.** liberty   **c.** beginning

3. A country has laws for _____ .
   a. justice   **b.** colors   **c.** stars

4. When a person is not afraid, he or she has _____ .
   a. songs   **b.** courage   **c.** states

5. Thick lines are _____ .
   a. flags   **b.** stars   **c.** stripes

6. The stars on the flag have a meaning. Each star _____ a state.
   a. joins   **b.** stands for   **c.** needs

COMPREHENSION

A. Looking for Main Ideas

Write complete answers to these questions.

1. What are the colors of the flag of the United States?

   _____

2. How many red and white stripes are there?

   _____

3. How many stars are there on the flag today?

   _____

B. Looking for Details

Circle T if the sentence is true. Circle F if the sentence is false.

	True	False
1. The national anthem is "The Stars and Stripes."	T	F
2. The United States was born in 1776.	T	F
3. There were thirteen states in the beginning.	T	F
4. In the beginning the flag had two colors.	T	F

	True	False
5. The color white is for courage.	T	F
6. The white stars are on a blue square.	T	F
7. Each new state gets a new stripe.	T	F
8. The last star was for Hawaii.	T	F

GRAMMAR

Complete the sentences with the correct article. Use *a* or *the*. If no article is necessary, write *X*.

EXAMPLE: The new country needed ___*a*___ flag.

1. _____ Stars and Stripes is a name for the flag.

2. _____ United States has a red, white, and blue flag.

3. _____ color red is for courage.

4. For each new state there is _____ new star.

5. Today, _____ flag has fifty stars.

6. There are _____ thirteen red and white stripes on the flag.

DISCUSSION

Discuss the answers to these questions with your classmates.

1. Describe another flag that you know.
2. What do people use flags for?
3. Design a flag for your school or class and say what it means.

INTRODUCING THE USA

Washington
Oregon
Montana
Idaho
North
Dakota
Minnesota
New
Hampshire
Maine
Vermont
Wyoming
South
Dakota
Wisconsin
Massachusetts
Michigan
New York
Rhode
Island
Nevada
Utah
Nebraska
Iowa
Illinois
Indiana
Ohio
Pennsylvania
Connecticut
New
Jersey
California
Colorado
Kansas
Missouri
West
Virginia
Virginia
Delaware
Maryland
Arizona
New Mexico
Oklahoma
Arkansas
Kentucky
Tennessee
North
Carolina
South
Carolina
Texas
Mississippi
Alabama
Georgia
Louisiana
Florida

Alaska

Hawaii

ANSWER KEY

UNIT 1

Vocabulary
1. nation **2.** union **3.** flat land **4.** climate
5. population **6.** origin **7.** emblem
8. its identity

Looking for Main Ideas
1. b **2.** a **3.** c

Looking for Details
1. ~~mountain~~/flower **2.** ~~Hawaii~~/Alaska
3. ~~people~~/names **4.** ~~Hawaii~~/Alaska
5. ~~nation~~/state **6.** ~~states~~/cities

Grammar
1. X **2.** a **3.** X **4.** The **5.** The **6.** X

UNIT 2

Vocabulary
1. b **2.** a **3.** a **4.** b **5.** a **6.** b

Looking for Main Ideas
1. Where did the buffalo live?
2. Who killed the buffalo for their hides?
3. How many buffalo are there in America today?

Looking for Details
1. F **2.** F **3.** F **4.** T **5.** T **6.** F

Grammar
1. of **2.** for **3.** with **4.** of **5.** in **6.** to

UNIT 3

Vocabulary
1. Texan **2.** ranch **3.** describe
4. produce **5.** mixture **6.** proud
7. probably **8.** boots

Looking for Main Ideas
1. a **2.** c **3.** a

Looking for Details
1. T **2.** T **3.** T **4.** F **5.** T **6.** F

Grammar
1. rode **2.** brought **3.** wore
4. took **5.** became **6.** built

UNIT 4

Vocabulary
1. a **2.** b **3.** b **4.** b **5.** a **6.** b

Looking for Main Ideas
1. a **2.** b **3.** c

Looking for Details
1. ~~nut~~/jar **2.** ~~snack~~/jelly **3.** ~~regular~~/healthy
4. ~~1980~~/1890 **5.** ~~nut~~/food
6. ~~patients~~/children **7.** ~~manufacturer~~/doctor
8. ~~sandwich~~/paste

Grammar
1. in **2.** into **3.** for **4.** from **5.** in **6.** for

UNIT 5

Vocabulary
1. resident **2.** U.S. citizen **3.** term
4. serve **5.** earn **6.** expenses
7. a limousine **8.** in fact

Looking for Main Ideas
1. You can be president for two terms of four years.
2. You earn $200,000 a year as president of the United States.
3. Twenty-two presidents were lawyers.

Looking for Details
1. ~~forty-five~~/thirty-five **2.** ~~lawyer~~/resident
3. ~~eight~~/four **4.** ~~two~~/three **5.** ~~teacher~~/college
6. ~~businessman~~/head

Grammar
1. Four presidents were soldiers.
2. Two presidents were writers.
3. Two presidents were businessmen.
4. Eight presidents did not have a college education.
5. They are presidents of the United States.

UNIT 6

Vocabulary
1. clergyman 2. assassin 3. protest
4. marches 5. violence 6. equality

Looking for Main Ideas
1. a 2. a 3. c

Looking for Details
1. F 2. T 3. F
4. T 5. F 6. T

Grammar
1. in 2. at 3. in 4. to 5. for 6. of

UNIT 7

Vocabulary
1. a 2. b 3. c 4. b 5. a 6. b 7. b
8. c

Looking for Main Ideas
1. b 2. a 3. c

Looking for Details
1. ~~ten~~/nine 2. ~~gym~~/soccer
3. ~~American~~/Canadian 4. ~~balls~~/baskets
5. ~~first~~/greatest or shortest 6. ~~climb~~/run

Grammar
1. in 2. on 3. with 4. of 5. up 6. from

UNIT 8

Vocabulary
1. b 2. c 3. b 4. b 5. a 6. a

Looking for Main Ideas
1. Everybody liked Abraham Lincoln because he was intelligent and hard-working.
2. Lincoln became president in 1860.
3. The North won the Civil War.

Looking for Details
1. F 2. T 3. F 4. T
5. T 6. F 7. F 8. T

Grammar
1. on 2. between 3. on 4. behind 5. in
6. of

UNIT 9

Vocabulary
1. a 2. a 3. b 4. b 5. a 6. a

Looking for Main Ideas
1. b 2. a 3. c

Looking for Details
1. T 2. F 3. F 4. F 5. T 6. F

Grammar
1. the 2. a 3. X 4. the 5. the 6. The

UNIT 10

Vocabulary
1. saints 2. scare 3. masks 4. skeletons
5. ghosts 6. play tricks

Looking for Main Ideas
1. b 2. b 3. a

Looking for Details
1. F 2. T 3. T 4. T 5. F 6. F

Grammar
1. on 2. in 3. into 4. with 5. from
6. for

UNIT 11

Vocabulary
1. b 2. a 3. b 4. a 5. b 6. b

Looking for Main Ideas
1. c 2. a 3. b

Looking for Details
1. F 2. F 3. T 4. T 5. T 6. T

Grammar
1. thought 2. believed 3. fought 4. lost
5. gave 6. made

UNIT 12

Vocabulary
1. a 2. b 3. a 4. b 5. b 6. b 7. a
8. a

Looking for Main Ideas
1. b 2. b 3. b

Looking for Details
3, 8, 1, 6, 7, 2, 5, 4

Grammar
1. was 2. made 3. played 4. loved
5. sent 6. wanted

UNIT 13

Vocabulary
1. b 2. a 3. b 4. a 5. b 6. a

Looking for Main Ideas
1. b 2. b 3. b

Looking for Details
1. T 2. T 3. T 4. F 5. F 6. T

Grammar
1. Other kinds of corn do not have 14 percent water.
2. Other kinds of corn do not pop.
3. Popcorn does not pop in water.
4. Today, people do not eat popcorn for Thanksgiving.
5. Popcorn at the movies is not popular in every country.
6. Movie theaters in the United States do not sell sweet corn.

UNIT 14

Vocabulary
1. celebrities 2. unusual 3. public parking
4. An attendant 5. jewelry 6. an elegant

Looking for Main Ideas
1. b 2. c 3. a

Looking for Details
1. stores/courts 2. sports/small 3. small/high
4. celebrity/attendant 5. 200,000/35,000
6. jewelry/maps

Grammar
1. of 2. for 3. around 4. in 5. on
6. for

UNIT 15

Vocabulary
1. rancher 2. nickname 3. asthma
4. energetic 5. an explorer 6. to hunt

Looking for Main Ideas
1. b 2. a 3. b

Looking for Details
1. T 2. T 3. F 4. F 5. T 6. F

Grammar
1. from 2. in 3. with 4. after 5. for
6. to

UNIT 16

Vocabulary
1. a 2. b 3. a 4. a 5. b 6. a

Looking for Main Ideas
1. b 2. c 3. a

Looking for Details
1. T 2. F 3. F 4. T 5. T 6. F

Grammar
1. on 2. in 3. out 4. down 5. for
6. away

UNIT 17

Vocabulary
1. b 2. b 3. b 4. a
5. c 6. b 7. b 8. a

Looking for Main Ideas
1. b 2. a 3. c

Looking for Details
1. F 2. T 3. F 4. T 5. T 6. F

Grammar
1. were 2. sold 3. escaped 4. took
5. hid 6. decided 7. became 8. went

UNIT 18

Vocabulary
1. b 2. c 3. a 4. c
5. b 6. c 7. a 8. b

Looking for Main Ideas
1. b 2. a 3. a

Looking for Details
1. Queen/King 2. leaders/soldiers
3. King/Jefferson 4. bells/guns
5. kings/picnics 6. state/country

Grammar
1. were 2. wanted 3. started
4. won 5. chose 6. signed

UNIT 19

Vocabulary
1. a 2. b 3. c 4. b
5. a 6. a 7. c 8. c

Looking for Main Ideas
1. a 2. b 3. c

Looking for Details
1. ~~California~~/the world 2. ~~old~~/high
3. ~~tannin~~/base 4. ~~American~~/alphabet
5. ~~fire~~/tannin 6. ~~president~~/naturalist
7. ~~people~~/sequoias 8. ~~presidential~~/national

Grammar
1. John Muir was a famous naturalist.
2. The General Sherman tree is 100 feet around its base.
3. The bark has a special juice.
4. Muir wanted to save the sequoias.
5. Sequoias never die from fire or disease.
6. John Muir studied plants and animals.

UNIT 20

Vocabulary
1. blind 2. deaf 3. Braille 4. an article
5. graduate 6. repeat 7. an illness
8. honors

Looking for Main Ideas
1. b 2. a 3. c

Looking for Details
3, 5, 2, 1, 7, 8, 4, 6

Grammar
1. worked 2. took 3. learned
4. repeated 5. read 6. wrote

UNIT 21

Vocabulary
1. b 2. a 3. c 4. c 5. a 6. b

Looking for Main Ideas
1. b 2. b 3. c

Looking for Details
1. ~~eleven~~/seven 2. ~~four~~/five
3. ~~Liberty~~/Broadway 4. ~~1960s~~/1920s
5. ~~ships~~/stores 6. ~~plays~~/ships

Grammar
1. the 2. The 3. X 4. a 5. the 6. a

UNIT 22

Vocabulary
1. a 2. b 3. a 4. c 5. c 6. c 7. b
8. b

Looking for Main Ideas
1. b 2. b 3. a

Looking for Details
1. T 2. T 3. F 4. T 5. F 6. F

Grammar
1. with 2. to 3. on 4. on 5. in 6. from

UNIT 23

Vocabulary
1. invent 2. laboratory 3. nap 4. closet
5. hired 6. light bulb

Looking for Main Ideas
1. b 2. a 3. c

Looking for Details
7, 4, 1, 6, 2, 3, 5

Grammar
1. invented 2. made 3. sold 4. hired
5. worked 6. took

UNIT 24

Vocabulary
1. figure 2. halls 3. stories 4. get lost
5. Navy 6. rings 7. maps 8. includes

Looking for Main Ideas
1. a 2. b 3. c

Looking for Details
1. F 2. T 3. T 4. F 5. F 6. T

Grammar
1. near 2. of 3. on 4. with 5. in 6. in

UNIT 25

Vocabulary
1. b 2. a 3. b 4. a 5. b 6. b

Looking for Main Ideas
1. a 2. b 3. c

Looking for Details
1. F 2. T 3. T 4. F 5. F 6. T

Grammar

1. spoke 2. started 3. enjoyed 4. passed
5. believed 6. said

UNIT 26

Vocabulary

1. a 2. b 3. a 4. b 5. a 6. a 7. b
8. a

Looking for Main Ideas

1. You see cheerleaders at sports events.
2. Johnny Campbell was the first cheerleader.
3. Cheerleaders work in teams.

Looking for Details

1. ~~pyramid~~/team 2. ~~dress~~/dance
3. ~~dance~~/game 4. ~~girls~~/men 5. ~~men~~/women
6. ~~pyramid~~/crowd

Grammar

1. in 2. of 3. until 4. from 5. on 6. for

UNIT 27

Vocabulary

1. b 2. b 3. a 4. b 5. b 6. a

Looking for Main Ideas

1. People go to a national park to enjoy nature.
2. Yellowstone became a national park in 1872.

3. Two-and-a-half million people visit Yellowstone each year.

Looking for Details

1. b 2. b 3. b 4. b 5. a 6. b

Grammar

1. There are geysers.
2. There are national parks.
3. Park rangers give information to visitors.
4. Park rangers take care of the parks.
5. National parks are large pieces of land.
6. Rangers tell visitors not to pick the flowers.

UNIT 28

Vocabulary

1. c 2. b 3. a 4. b 5. c 6. b

Looking for Main Ideas

1. The colors of the flag are red, white, and blue.
2. There are thirteen red and white stripes.
3. There are fifty stars on the flag today.

Looking for Details

1. F 2. T 3. T 4. F 5. F 6. T
7. F 8. T

Grammar

1. The 2. The 3. The 4. a 5. the 6. X

Photo Credits for *Introducing the USA*

Page 4   Buffalo–National Park Service Photograph

Page 16   Martin Luther King, Jr.–The Martin Luther King, Jr., Center for Nonviolent Social Change, Inc., Atlanta, Georgia

Page 19   Basketball–Courtesy of the New York Knicks, New York, NY

Page 22   Abraham Lincoln–National Portrait Gallery, Smithsonian Institution, Washington, D.C.

Page 25   Washington, D.C., Collage–Washington, D.C., Convention and Visitors Association

Page 31   Native Americans–Smithsonian Institution, Washington, D.C.

Page 34   Shirley Temple–From CHILD STAR, by Shirley Temple Black, McGraw-Hill, 1976; Twentieth Century Fox Photo

Page 43   Theodore Roosevelt–Smithsonian Institution, Washington, D.C.

Page 49   Harriet Tubman–Anacostia Museum, Smithsonian Institution, Washington, D.C.

Page 52   July Fourth Fireworks–Fireworks by Grucci, Brookhaven, NY

Page 55   Sequoias–National Park Service Photograph

Page 58   Helen Keller–Courtesy of the Perkins School for the Blind, Watertown, MA

Page 61   New York City Skyline–New York Convention & Visitors Bureau

Page 67   Thomas A. Edison–Smithsonian Institution, Washington, D.C.

Page 70   The Pentagon–Washington, D.C., Convention & Visitors Association

Page 73   Jaime Escalante–A/P Wide World Photos

Page 79   Yellowstone National Park–National Park Service Photograph